JEAN MEYER

THROUGH
THE GATE

A CHILDHOOD HOME REVISITED

JEAN MEYER

THROUGH
THE GATE

A CHILDHOOD HOME REVISITED

MEREO
Cirencester

Mereo Books

1A The Wool Market Dyer Street Cirencester Gloucestershire GL7 2PR
An imprint of Memoirs Publishing www.mereobooks.com

Through the gate: 978-1-86151-481-3

First published in Great Britain in 2015
by Mereo Books, an imprint of Memoirs Publishing

The address for Memoirs Publishing Group Limited can be found at
www.memoirspublishing.com

The Memoirs Publishing Group Ltd Reg. No. 7834348

The Memoirs Publishing Group supports both The Forest Stewardship Council® (FSC®) and
the PEFC® leading international forest-certification organisations. Our books carrying both the
FSC label and the PEFC® and are printed on FSC®-certified paper. FSC® is the only
forest-certification scheme supported by the leading environmental organisations including
Greenpeace. Our paper procurement policy can be found at
www.memoirspublishing.com/environment

Typeset in 11.5/17pt Bembo
by Wiltshire Associates Publisher Services Ltd. Printed and bound in
Great Britain by Printondemand-Worldwide, Peterborough PE2 6XD

Through the unknown, remembered gate
When the last of earth left to discover
Is that which was the beginning.

T.S. Eliot, Little Gidding

for Ken
his children
and grandchildren

CONTENTS

THE FIRST DREAM

Walking down the street, I came upon it suddenly, taken by surprise because being entirely white it had seemed like a space, an emptiness between two other houses. Even the windows were whitened over; it was as if a giant brush had swept right over it. I walked up to the door and mother opened it: an old grey-haired woman but happy, smiling, welcoming. We embraced. On walking back to the gate, I saw there was a note fixed to it: *Buy my house.*

GOING HOME
WITH GOOGLE

It was hard to be sure at first which one it was, but I had memories to help me, like being able to see the lamp-post from my bedroom window, and the place where the Crescent begins to turn on the opposite side of the road. After peering at the numbers, not always visible, and using the arrows to move slowly along the road, I found it. I gazed, and felt the quickened beat of my heart.

They have painted the pebble-dash white and the bricks redder than they were, and within the porch, a lasting, sensible structure of brick, there is a white door where once - oh so long ago - there was a green door with a round window in it. The windows upstairs and down no longer open like a book but with a flap, in the top part only. The little front garden with two round bushes and a hedge and roses is all gone, concreted over so that the owner can drive his car off the road and park it under his own window, deeming this to be a better view than a bit of green. There are vertical blinds at the windows to stop people looking in, and perhaps the owner never looks out anyway; what would there be to see?

The only things outside in the empty concrete space, partly closed off from the pavement by a flimsy fence with a hole in it, are three recycling bins, and I see that all the houses have them out there at the front. Our grey, galvanized bins (no recycling) used to be in the back garden out of sight, and were serviced by the council vehicles that drove along the back alley. Now I suppose they won't manoeuvre down the alley and have some contract or by-law that obliges people to place their rubbish on view in easily-accessible areas where the wheeled bins can be pushed in and out without effort, never mind the ugliness of it. How I would love to see the back garden, but Google won't show it to me.

As my eye wandered over every detail, as I used the arrows to move my viewpoint, I had another wish – to go to primary school once again. Would Google take me there?

I set off along the street, clicking my way to the end of it, recalling bit by bit what would follow on. At the end of the street I was given an option to proceed – "click on the square to go there" – and I found myself on the way to primary school, half a century on. Turn right and down this long road that leads to the docks, once part of one of the greatest ports of Europe. Where there were green fields ("the farmer's field" we called the one where there was a pond with tadpoles), now there are only factories and warehouses and offices. In the Fifties when I used to walk down here to school there was only one large factory, there on the right, and I remember it was at the gate of this factory that I saw my first black man in the flesh. I stopped in my tracks (what was I - seven, eight? - we didn't even have a television yet) and was afraid to pass, and I remember how he said to me -"What's the matter? You want to pass? Pass then, I won't hurt you."

Now, here on the left, there is a line of trees and a wall, beyond which there must be the village, with the village school and its green. If there is the wall, there must be the gate I went through each day. I'm rushing now, I'm clicking too fast and I come to a road that goes left, where no road should be. Backtracking, I find the wall again, but it is broken off suddenly; they have broken through the wall to make the road. I have a vivid memory of the gate that used to be the only entrance into the enclosed village - a tall, wooden green gate with a clicking latch, and once through it I seemed to be in another world made up of green spaces and merry little houses and a silence broken only by the sound of footsteps. I travel on along the wall, and here is a gap in it, with two brick pillars on each side: the gate is gone, perished wood, but the brick remains with the iron fixings for the hinges, and now I am astonished to see that it is not a high wall at all, an adult could lean on it; it must have only seemed high to my small self. I am amused and deeply moved by this discovery.

Will Google take me on? Yes it will, there are not many

options because the streets are few here, but it takes me on - along the road, not through the gap in the wall of course - and there, on the corner, is the school, just the same as it always was, a splendid stocky little Victorian edifice in the dark stone of the north. They have painted the railings and the window frames in a startling bright blue which leaps out against the brown stone and makes it look merry. I find I can travel about it a bit, look at it from different angles; here we went in, here we played hopscotch and skipping, here a boy hit me in the chest and made me cry and over there, across the road on the green, in our last year, Mr Lewis took us to plant trees, one for each of us, perhaps in the hope that we would grow strong and tall with them.

I can see the trees - a great green cloud along the edge of the field - but Google will not take me to the trees; it is not interested in sentimental greenery, only in roads and buildings. I turn back to the school and read the board that bears its name, but I know, because I have already checked it out, that the decision was made two years ago to close it because of insufficient intake.

Little ghosts run about the playground, ribbons in their hair and woolly long socks on their little legs, shouting and skipping and swinging on the railings.

No more. All gone, as we say to infants. Look, all gone.

I retrace my steps to home, and look again.

This is where I started life, quite literally, rushing into the world one cold January night, not in a warm hospital theatre but upstairs in that unheated bedroom (that one up there with the two panes that used to be four). I left this house very young, running hard and not looking back to wave, whitening it out with one broad brushstroke, and here I am now, forty years on, creeping back to peer at it, at all of us, holding my breath as though I were an intruder.

Just imagine if I were to buy it, this modest little house that dozens have passed through on their way 'up the ladder'; suppose I were to close the circle and after all my wanderings, end my days where I began them, in those rooms, upon those stairs, in that garden; suppose I were to hang up all my paintings on the walls, wipe out the sorrow, restore the colour, give the place back to its rightful occupants? Fifty years is a long time to call a house Home, when it wasn't even their own property.

APPROACHING

Two paths, front and back. We always said *down* the path, going out, and *up* the path coming in, as if we lived on a hill.

Down the path you walk to your freedom, you go off to discover the world out there, to seek your fortune, as it said in my books of tales. Off you go, whistling, with your hands in your pockets and a few things tied up in a handkerchief. And up the path you return to seek your consolation, your comfort, when the world outside is too hard to cope with. You open the gate and the path runs away before you to the door where there should be a smiling face with welcoming arms outstretched to receive you, but sometimes the door doesn't open, the curtains are drawn and only dread draws your feet along.

THE BACK PATH

Fifteen metres of concrete ran straight from the kitchen door to the wooden gate which opened and closed with a small latch that you could see moving up and down to announce somebody's entrance, if you were looking out of the window. The green gate was let into a high wall made of massive dark stone bricks, and beyond the wall was the lane, which we called 'the back entry', shortened to 'the entry'. Running the whole length of the entry on both sides and curving slightly, just there, outside our gate, it was not a dank narrow passage, such as they like to show in films about northern poverty, nor was it wide enough to be a viable road. It sometimes caught the sun; children played safely there and you could walk, or cycle, along it, to go to the shops or the bus stop. The green wooden gates were all alike, opening onto strips of back garden, some carefully tended, others used as rubbish deposits, each faithfully reflecting the natures of those within the house walls.

The path did not divide our garden into two equal parts: on one side was a narrow strip of grass that served no purpose in its mean width and a flimsy fence separating us from the neighbour, while on the other side of the path was the garden as such, divided in its turn by a large bush. In front of the bush was the 'lawn', a grand name for a few steps of grass which father mowed meticulously and where, on rare summer days, deckchairs were unfolded for the English thrill of Sitting Outside. Here also, mother had her 'rockery': a little slope leaning against the coal shed where she tried to recreate in miniature the larger compositions she'd seen in the seaside town parks, using stones and bits of broken brick, and tiny red-capped gnomes that peeped out among the greenery. Here, when he retired and was still in command of his mind, in that brief space of time, father got to work with slats of wood and gave her his masterpiece, something she'd probably always wanted - a bower of roses. Somehow, all by himself, he raised up a bridge-like criss-cross structure and started growing roses over it. I have still today a tiny square photograph of mother sitting in her deckchair beneath the ripe blooms, while father clicks the shutter to fix that moment like a proof. *Look, I gave her a rose garden.* What more could she want?

Behind the bush, the garden was left to itself. Nothing was planted, nobody went there for any reason, unless just to recover a ball, or to put something in the bin that stood next to the gate for the convenience of the binmen (who are now the ecological operators who dictate that the bins must be at the front of the house). The grass grew long here, was known intimately only by the cat, and was dealt with only sporadically by father.

Beneath the long grass and weeds, so I was told when small, were the remains of the air raid shelter. A couple of rusty lengths of corrugated metal languished for a few years against the wall and then they disappeared, leaving no visible trace of this thing whose name was full of mystery for me, because I was the only one who had never been inside it, indeed, never seen it. While father was out with the ambulances, they must have been fairly often inside it, mother, Ida, Doreen and baby Ken, so close to the port as they were; sitting there in the dark, not knowing if they would have a house to go back into, or be buried there alive all together. Perhaps it was these associations that led them to ignore that part of the garden altogether. "That dreadful wilderness", mother used to call it, within father's hearing.

The Bottom of the Garden became a mythical place to my mind, full of unseen mysteries and, all too soon, the buried remains of the cat were added to it. If, coming home from school, I chanced to come in by the back way, I rushed up the path as if all the hounds of Hell were after me.

"I wish you'd shut that gate properly," mother said.

After his retirement, father, for whom life had been a matter of precision, proportion and programming, shoes polished and hands out of pockets, went into his own final wilderness of mind and that wild shaggy place in the garden that he had kept in reserve, where his demons sat chuckling in the long grass waiting for him to throw off his tie and dance with them, began to spread towards the house. Mother was left alone, the mower rusted away in the shed and the roses, after a brief season of chaos, withered and fell down.

There is another picture taken in this garden. I have it still; two inches square and grey, as they all used to be. The moment lives in my memory still, after nearly sixty years. It must have been Sunday, because we were all there together. The day was warm and the kitchen door left open for people to wander in and out. I was playing on the grass with some little moon-shaped thing (I can see it in my hand in the picture), talking to the ants, picking the grass blades, hopping on the path, immersed in a world of tiny happinesses. Doreen, in plaits, passed by with her bicycle on her way down to the back lane , and my other sister Ida, who was so much older than me that I knew her only vaguely as another woman in the house with mother, was sunbathing in a deckchair with her face all shiny and her legs bare. She was in her first office job, going off to work in the morning and off to dance in the evening, so I could be barely aware of her existence, except on Sundays. Mother was, of course, somewhere in the dimness of the kitchen and occasionally there would be callings from indoor to outside and perhaps Ida would go in for a while and come back later. Father was standing in the garden smoking a pipe, quietly surveying his small tribe and bit of jungle.

Ken was still in short trousers, with those thick woollen socks, even in summer, that used to mark out English boys all over the world, and a short-sleeved white shirt. Father, proud of his new Kodak, saw a photo-opportunity and got him to sit in the fold-up chair with me.

"Sit down there with him."

"Come on, sit here with me."

Would I keep still long enough? The rough blue material of my pinafore dress bent into stiff folds as I leaned against my brother's knees and he put his arms around me and his cheek next to mine and 'click' the Kodak went, and then I was off again like a grasshopper.

Sunday afternoon, it must have been, because morning meant church. Off we went all together, spruced up and shiny, down the back path to catch the bus. The Methodist church was a building of massive stone just like that of the entry wall, and cold, almost always cold. I learned the word 'pew'. Tall windows, a great empty cross, shiny wood, stark simplicity; this was what a church meant to me then, and what I sometimes long for now, surrounded as I have been half my life by bleeding Christs, Madonnas with their Bambini and all the magnificent angels of the Renaissance. I would not be without this art for anything, but in the quiet emptiness of a Protestant church, with no seductive beauty to distract me, I can listen more closely perhaps, to what I need to know.

There was little to look at: the backs of people's heads and women's hats; a board with big blue numbers on it; the brown-backed little books with gold edged thin paper that were always lying in front of us when we went into the pew; a big wooden plate that was carried from pew to pew during the service, usually by a small man with a limp, into which everybody put coins. Mother gave me a penny, a big smooth penny of the Fifties, and I slipped it in. Some people put in little white envelopes, which mother despised. I learned another new word: 'pulpit'. Here the minister stood up and talked, and before I was old enough to follow his words, mother used to give me a little notepad and a pencil so that I could draw and keep myself quiet. So - my art began in the church.

But the best thing of all was the singing. Lots of it. The blue numbers told you which hymns we were going to sing, so that you could find your place in the brown book. *Abide With Me; Eternal Father, Strong to Save; Nearer My God To Thee…* Mother, who sang well, had favourites and dislikes and recognised them from the numbers, whispering to father, "He always plays that too slow."

Everyone sang, loud and robustly, including the old, off-key people who sat at the back and made me giggle. At the end, we filed out and people stood around the door for a few minutes if it wasn't too cold, to say hello and goodbye. So many people, only ever seen on a Sunday. I was a bit afraid of Flo, because she had big eyes that looked in opposite directions, but she always came up to us, limping with her orthopaedic boots. I thought then that Flo was old, but now

I realise she was probably about forty. These single women were dotted around my childhood, women who had lost their loves in the war and not found, or not wanted, anybody else. With skirts and hats that always seemed old-fashioned, as if time had stopped with the death of their men, they did their tiny shopping and walked little dogs. They taught in schools, they went to church, they were, in mother's words, left 'on the shelf': a dim dusty fate, or so it seemed.

Then, after a few years, mother began to stay at home on Sunday morning; she said she couldn't go to church and see to the lunch for six at the same time. Ida went off with friends for the day; Ken and Doreen slipped away too on various pretexts, so that in the end it was father and I who went off in our Sunday best, until I came to the conclusion, through debate with the RE teacher, that God wasn't there anyway. Father went off alone down the path after that, scarf folded tight, head held high, true to the last.

The latch of the gate could not only be seen as it bobbed up and down, but also heard from inside the house if there weren't other noises going on, so that it was almost impossible for someone to get to the back door before being noticed.

Clunk and here is father coming home with the Sunday ice-cream block.

Clunk and here is mother weighed down with shopping bags.

Clunk and here comes Ken with his bicycle and red knees.

Clunk and here come the Coal Men with their funny black and white faces.

No Clean Air Act in the Fifties. The coal was coal, not coke - heavy, dusty and black - and it came in jute sacks piled on an open lorry which, in my very earliest years, was pulled by a carthorse. The lorry wormed its way slowly along the back entry, stopping at each gate where there was a delivery to be made. *Clunk*, and one man came up the path to announce the delivery to my mother. She wiped her hands on her apron, gave the go-ahead and, for me peeping out of the living room window, the show began.

Looking out on the garden from the living room window, you could see, just below to the right a small, robust stone construction to which father had added an upper storey made of wood with a door that opened like that of a stable. No horse head appeared when you opened it - this was the Coal House. One by one the Coal Men carried the massive heavy sacks along the path, balanced on their backs and necks, which were protected by empty coal sacks worn like friars' hoods; with their arms and faces blackened by coal-dust and their white-circled eyes staring along the path, they seemed to me like figures from another world. On reaching the Coal House the Coal Man would pause for a second, shift the weight carefully forward and then empty the sack over his head into the dark interior. Only then did he straighten up and become a recognisable man again, folding up his empty sack neatly and sometimes even smiling at me through the window.

After only a few years of my childhood, the horse was replaced by a lorry, and after another few years, the Coal Men too disappeared, along with the coal, leaving us with stuff called Coke and synthetic firelighters that mother said were never as good as real wood. The end of the coal fire saw the end of another visitor to our home, who only came once a year, but when he did it was a drama. The chairs and table in the living room had to be covered with old sheets and the rug covered with layers of newspaper. Mother clucked around anxiously, hoping she wouldn't have 'much to clean up' and the taciturn Chimney Sweep tramped in with his long thin sticks. He was even more anonymous, in his dirt, than the Coal Men; his shirt, his trousers, his waistcoat, his face and the flat cap on his head were all the same dark non-colour. He was always alone and said almost nothing, kneeling down in front of the fireplace to fix his long sticks one into the other.

"Go out the back and watch it come out!" mother would say. So I ran down the path a little way and raised my face to the roof, where the brick chimneys stood against the sky. Out of one of these there suddenly popped a round black brushhead, which looked like a puppet bird bowing to the public, turning quickly this way and that before all at once being sucked back into the chimney as if someone had pulled it by the legs. What a show! What a lot of fun, to have been caused by that unlikely, silent, grimy man.

The window cleaner was not grimy but always silent. Up the path he came with the wonderful ladder that grew longer and longer as I watched it; his visits were arranged in advance on a regular basis and he was paid once a month, so it didn't even matter if, when he arrived, mother happened to be out for a moment, as he did his work and went on to the next customer. This strange face at the window, looking in on us, at all our things (so I thought) was not something I liked at all, so I would try to be in another room all the time he was washing and rubbing.

One day, I was caught out in my sisters' bedroom; I had not heard the soft thud of his ladder against the wall. Looking in the dressing table mirror I was secretly playing with a lipstick and to my horror, behind my reflection the head and chest of the window cleaner slowly rose into view. Caught red-lipped, red-fingered, I sidled away into the bathroom as though the eye of God had glared upon me, as father had said it would.

The paths not only brought people in to us but were bridges to the outside world too, and every crossing, for a child, was an adventure, a breeze on the face, the feel of sunlight or rain and above all the excitement of a change of place, be it park or shop or playground. Going down the path through the back garden usually meant something nice. In the wild overgrown park, with its stream where Ken used to go fishing with his friends, and its upstairs-downstairs walks between the giant roots of trees and the red-iron rocks, there was a tunnel under the old railway bridge; a dank, dripping, echoing place that seemed infinitely long to my little legs.

The sun could not penetrate far inside and it was always muddy in the middle. On our Sunday afternoon walks father always had to carry me over the mud at that point, and feeling the odd prickliness of his jacket (so different from mother's soft cottons and wools), I watched the water trickling down the mossy, curved walls and listened to the quiet plopping of drops. The end of the tunnel was a miniscule semicircle of light in the darkness, and as we drew nearer I saw that the bright light was blotched with blue and green patches.

"Aaaah! Woooh!" My voice mocked me, rebounding from the walls. Nearer and nearer we got to the light until the patches resolved themselves into bushes and trees - but they were different, it seemed to me they had nothing to do with the part of the park we had left behind, the light on them was special. When he let me down on dry ground nor far from the exit, I stopped suddenly and gazed, spellbound.

"Look," I whispered, calling up images from my first story books, "it's *fairyland!*"

We came out onto the bluebell-dotted slopes under the tall trees and I did not run but moved about carefully in the sunshine, picking the flowers of an enchanted land, happy in my belief that small creatures, perhaps with wings, were watching me from under leaves and behind branches. Father clicked his Kodak camera - "Look here, look over here!"

Later, I ran up the path, breathless with anticipation, hair ribbon all awry, the bluebells already drooping in my hot fist, to where she, the queen on the hill, was working at the sink in her apron.

"These are for you!"

The beam on her face was the sun itself for me, both so rare in those parts, and her words were a blessing on me, just as precious. "Oh, for me?! Aren't they lovely, I'll put them in a cup, just here, where I can see them."

In the meagre British summer, father sometimes came up the path with a carton of ice cream, a great event, even though there were only ever three flavours – vanilla, chocolate and strawberry – side by side in a brick, called 'Neapolitan'. Or else the ice cream van came along the road with its instantly recognized jingle, and all the children ran down the front paths with their sixpences and shillings in their fists, down the path and straight into the road because cars passed at the rate of four or five a day.

THE FRONT PATH

The back path was functional; the front path was ceremonial. It was down the front path that we trooped, all of us except father and Ida because workers had to go to work whatever happened, to see the Queen. She was brand new, the Queen, and we all had little stiff Union Jack flags attached to balsa wood sticks that we had bought from Woolworths. We walked up the length of the road and then past the small row of shops to get to the main road, where people were already gathering side by side. It was a hot summer's day and the elastic in the sleeves of my dress was biting into my arms and I had to keep screwing up my eyes against the light. All around me there were legs and backs and women's skirts that kept wheeling round and all the chatter and laughter was going on above my head. Mother and Doreen urged, "Come on to the front, come here", but after a few minutes they forgot about me and the forest closed around me again.

There was a long time to wait. I fiddled with my flag and conjured up my picture of the Queen, a hybrid from the pictures in Grimm and Andersen: two, or maybe four, white horses with long tails and bells, pulling a golden coach; at the back of the coach, two pageboys standing and holding on, with pigtails and three-cornered hats; at the window, in satin lace and diamond splendour, wearing a sparkling crown, the Queen - looking out and waving a white-gloved hand to us. The Snow Queen! Perhaps she would bend gracefully down and sweep me up in her arm, take me to the cold palace to awaken, with my tears, a brother's frozen heart. Awaiting the incarnation of this vision, I was trembling with excitement and an odd kind of fear. My flag had slipped down the wooden stick with all my fiddling, and I began to whine because of this and because of the sun that was turning my upper arms bright pink.

"Here, have mine," said Ken, and he gave me his flag.

A little while longer and then there was a kind of distant murmur that grew stronger on its way to us like a wave, or a wind, and in the bustle of sudden activity I was thrust to the front again - "Get here! Get here!" - and with the forest of arms heaving above me I raised my little flag to and fro, looking for the horses.

A big black car slid between the two rows of people like a slug. It made no sound that you could hear above the noise of cheering, and for just a second I glimpsed, in a dim back window, a dark profile. Then it was gone. Arms and flags and voices all fell suddenly to a momentary stillness, followed by the murmur of people moving off home, their minds already on the simple necessities of the evening.

Perhaps the grown-ups were as disappointed as I was; if they were, they did not say so. Come to that, neither did I.

"Did you see her?"

"Yeah, 'course I did."

We all bravely pretended we were satisfied. On the way back to the relief of our ordinary tea things, our flags now just junk, only mother murmured a closing thought. "Eh well, when all's said and done, they're no better than us."

I thought a fairytale Queen was much superior to the real thing; perhaps that was the beginning of a preference for other worlds, of a longing to pass through mirrors, get through gates into a magic garden, follow a beckoning rabbit who-knows-where, and of a lasting confusion. Television was still some years away and sometimes we went to the cinema, where the seats were wooden and slippery and a woman hovered around with a tray of ice creams in paper tubs. The first film I ever saw in my life was *Bambi*. Mother took me in the afternoon and after we had been sitting for about twenty minutes we had to change seats because mother said there was a 'funny man' next to her. When Bambi could not wake his mother and lay down next to her lifeless body, I was filled with terror and whispered anxiously up to mother, "Is she *dead*, Mum, is she really *dead*?" and she whispered down to me, "Don't cry, lovey, it's only a film."

There were always two films for your ticket: the 'A' film (usually good) and the 'B' film (it didn't matter too much if you came in in the middle of it) and between the two there was a news feature or documentary. The rapid, clipped voice of the upper-class male commentator accompanied the black and white jerky films, sometimes with precarious background music.

After Bambi, that day, there was the film of the dead. There was no warning; suddenly, up there on the big screen, was an inexplicable scene. In some kind of yard, some large fenced enclosure, there were people: the living and the others. The living were standing about as if lost, or else, with scarves over their faces, carrying the 'others' from somewhere and throwing them onto a great heap of the same kind of 'others'. That was what I saw. I did not understand that those white 'things' being cast carelessly away like that were people; had been people. They were so thin and when they were thrown their arms and legs whirled disjointedly in all directions like those of old puppets or dolls. People were never like that. They couldn't have been people. I sat on the wooden cinema seat with my face turned up to the screen and my mouth open. The commentary quacked away and it meant nothing to me, yet by the time it was over the suspicion that the puppets were people had wormed its way into my mind, not least of all through mother's silence. She did not lean down to me in the dark and whisper "*It's only a film*".

Pinocchio I saw with father, who took the opportunity to

make it a lesson in life. When the cricket sings "*and always let your conscience be your guide*", he leaned down to me and whispered out of the corner of his mouth, "That's good advice. You want to remember that".

If there were no films to see at the cinema, or if it was raining, my hands were always occupied with something: paper dolls had to be cut out of a comic, together with their paper clothes, which had tabs on the shoulders and sides to fold around the figure in its modest underwear, played with for half an hour and then their flat flimsy lives forgotten; dots to be joined up, figures to be coloured in, boxes to be glued into existence (the fascination of discovering that a box began its life as a flat drawing! For a whole afternoon I did nothing but draw them, cut them out and stick them together – *Look, look I've made a BOX!*)

There was a farmhouse too, with small white fences and tiny sheep, cows and pigs to herd about, all made of painted lead, plastic not yet having won the day, but the best thing of all was the Doll's House. I could open the side of it and there they all were, the rooms and the minuscule, perfect furniture, even down to the potty under the bed. Fingers could reach in and decide the state of play, the fate of each tiny figure in the chairs, on the stairs or in the beds, leaning out of the windows, sitting at the table in the kitchen. Their days were mine to command, their lives literally in my hands to manipulate in godlike fashion. As an adult, watching news reports of earthquakes in which the sides of houses have been ripped away, leaving the modest contents of bedrooms exposed to the gaze of the world - shabby cupboards and poor little framed pictures askew on the walls - my mind returns to that early tiny world that I could open and close at will and make it as I wanted it.

On the first day that I was allowed to get up and get dressed, after my long infant illness, it was warm summer weather and in the afternoon mother opened the front door and let me walk to the end of the path - "just to the end, mind you, and then come back again" - to put some fresh air back in my lungs. As I stood there on the pavement, obediently not taking another step while I looked along the street, father called my name and clicked his Kodak just as I turned my face towards him. There I am still, in a tiny square grey photograph, a little skinny figure with tired eyes, half-turned to the camera, the long afternoon shadows slicing the empty road behind me. Whatever it was that had wanted to cut me down in my first green leafing, it had failed; I had won my right to life. Off down that path I would go every morning after that, down the street and a good twenty minute walk to school, through fields with the sounds of ships not far away. The first morning in the classroom, when she turned to go and I thought it was forever, I clung so hard to her old brown coat that Miss Powell had to pry my fingers loose.

I had never been away from her; each afternoon after lunch we had sat together near the radio - she with her knitting, me with my hands around my knees - for twenty minutes of *Listen With Mother*. It had to be *with* mother, I was adamant about it, if she delayed in the kitchen I called her, "It's *staaarting!*"

To stop my screaming Miss Powell got all the children in a circle on chairs and started a song that involved actions: "*under the spreading chest* (touch chest) *nut* (touch head) *treeee*" (arms up and out). I sat with my hands in the lap of my tartan skirt, but by the end of the song I had raised my arms too. At four o'clock, mother waiting behind the railings seemed already a normal thing and I had forgotten the end of the world a few hours ago.

This small village school with three teachers and about two hundred children, for some reason unknown to me, was not the school my brother was going to, so it was a new world which I entered alone and without the daily companionship of getting there and home again, which might have kept alive that bond, fixed in the garden photograph, which was so soon to unravel and slip away.

When I was old enough to walk there alone, the journey itself became the first interest of the day. Among the fields there were only one or two factories then, the long road that led eventually down to the docks was still bordered by hedges, and children could safely get to the school without fear of traffic. The village was one of those creations that were set up by enterprising Victorians for housing their workers and providing them with sanitary conditions, surrounding greenery and a place for recreation in their free time. It was closed off from the road by a red brick wall and when I went through the gate it seemed to me that I was entering an enchanted place like in one of my stories, with greener grass, redder roofs and brighter sunshine. All day long I wrote and read and drew and sang and struggled with numbers; jumped about in the playground like all the other grasshoppers; drank my little bottle of milk (frozen solid sometimes in the winter); ate my free lunch from the thick white plates; wrote and read and drew some more, then passed again through the gate onto the road that led me home to ordinariness.

"She's got a head on her shoulders, that one," said father, within hearing of my brother, unravelling already the first strands of that bond. My brother was never to take my hand any more.

A few years later, Ken had his own money, from his first job, and his own key, a great conquest. We hardly ever saw each other any more, crossing paths awkwardly in the hall sometimes, he in his work dungarees and me in my Grammar School uniform. There never seemed anything to say; I knew nothing of his life nor he of mine. One afternoon, the bus I was on passed by the big gates of the shipyard just as the first lot of workers were spilling out, hundreds of men that in only a few more years would be reduced to a sorry trickle and then the big gates would close forever. In the "you've-never-had-it-so-good" days it was easy to get a job: Doreen and Ida typed away their teens in whatever offices they chose to apply to, and Ken slipped into a place in the shipyard as easily as the ships going down to the water. If you didn't like your job you could say 'I'm off!'", give your notice on a Monday and start in a new place the next Monday. This helped to mask the fact that Ken could not 'stick at' anything – it always seemed to end in a quarrel, resentment, going off in a huff. But for a short while there was always a bit of money in his pocket, and he was deep in the initiation ceremonies of his peers, involving rounds of drinks in the pub and packets of ciggies offered. He was a shy boy, because of his stammer, and there were no other ways that he knew of making friends, and after the lonely desert of school that was what he needed more than anything.

More often than not, he came home smelling of beer, and while that was the norm in most other houses, in the house of a Methodist teetotaller it was a signal for high tension. You could almost hear it in the air: a quivering elastic that was being slowly stretched to breaking point. One night he was particularly late, and mother was having a silent contest with father to see who would not go to bed first. She would not leave them alone together. She pottered about in the kitchen – "I'll just do the veg for tomorrow, that'll save me time" – while he sat in his armchair pretending to still be watching the late news, but I knew that both of them were waiting, ears straining, for that key-in-lock signal. They were so preoccupied that I was forgotten and as nobody told me to go to bed, I didn't; I sat curled up behind a *Girl's Annual*.

The front door opened with a click and that elastic gave

a great 'twang'. The trouble was, he was swaying - if he hadn't been swaying, everyone might have gone to bed in relative peace, but one look at him leaning against the wall, smiling, and all father's teetotal Wesleyan upbringing came rushing with the blood into his head, and the elastic broke.

"I won't have it in my house! Don't you dare come home in that state!"

Father spoke with his rage battened down, terrifying. As always, she stood between them, her face working in the effort of peacemaker and her fingers working that apron that she never seemed to take off. The little stuffy room seemed to shrink even smaller and I did everything I could to do the same, clinging to my open book, my heart pounding.

"He's not that bad, he's only had a few, he's quite sensible…"

Mother tried to calm the waters. But that smile seemed to fan father's rage.

"I'll bolt the door on you!"

There was a funny kind of snort and then Ken said, straightening up a moment, "All right then!" And suddenly he was off like a shot, fumbling with the front door latch a moment and then gone into the night. Oblivious to the cold, mother ran down the path in her apron and slippers and in the doorway I was suddenly afraid that she, too, would vanish into the darkness and never return. There she was, fixed in the pool of lamplight at the end of the path, her face looking yellow and awful, calling up the street,

"Ken! *Ken!*"

"*Mummy!*"

My cry was no less desperate, but although she came back in, she walked slowly past me like a sleep-walker, as if I were invisible.

How long was that front path? A few yards, not more, but, fifteen years old and dressed in a bridesmaid's blue outfit, clutching a bouquet and feeling that I made a rotten bridesmaid because I wore glasses, it seemed a mile to me. On the day Ida was married, everybody was up two hours earlier than usual, and the house seemed to have double the number of people in it, so busy were they going from one room to another, dressing and redressing and checking other people's dress, losing and finding things, worrying and laughing. I had strange hair, used Doreen's lipstick with permission and was afraid to sit down in the wide blue skirt of my dress. People were constantly going up and down stairs and the bathroom was never free.

At last, the hired cars arrived and the green front door with its round window like a porthole was opened. To my astonishment, there were neighbours at the end of the path, three or four on each side, and when Doreen and I went out to our car, there was an odd silence. I could feel their eyes upon me, although I did not have the courage to look at them but almost ran, as if I thought they might hit me as I passed.

We were not much loved. It was known that in our Methodist household "you can't even have a drink", and although mother had her friends in the street, being of an open and sociable nature, father was unfortunate in that he had a facial expression which, in repose, seemed to be supercilious, and a way of walking, hands always out of pockets, that made it seem as if he was in a procession.

He had no friends. I once came across an official photograph of him standing with his work apprentices in the technical drawing office - it was the standard pose of all school photographs: three rows of boys, two standing and the front one sitting, all in identical overalls, and father standing to one side in a white coat, his round glasses glinting with the light, his mouth slightly open in the way he considered proper when being photographed. The boys, you can tell somehow from their faces, were respectful, but not affectionate. They would always have said 'sir' and would probably not have asked questions, nor delayed their exit at the end of the sessions. Father would have died rather than enter a pub, so the only other men he knew were his church colleagues, and nobody ever came to the house, except for the boyfriends of Doreen and Ida.

They always came up the front path, too, wiping their feet laboriously on the mat and stepping into the hallway, where they seemed to be too big, too loud to fit in to our crowded little household. Harry, later Ida's husband, was the most relaxed; he wore casual tweedy jackets and I looked forward to his visits because, for some reason, he always pressed a half-crown into my palm, as if he were bribing me to keep silent about something he had done, or might do. Ida would trot down the path with him to his little yellow Beetle parked conspicuously in the empty road and off they would go for the afternoon to the coast, or for the evening to the city dance hall. Jack, who never became Doreen's husband, sat in a dark suit and looked around him with a certain discomfort, as though he suspected hidden germs about to cling to him. He was always polite to mother and father, but I disliked him because he had a red skin that looked as if he was always scrubbing at it, and because he ignored me entirely. Mother's reserves were linked to the two facts that he was from the south and he was a Catholic.

"That Cockney twang," she would say, out of Doreen's hearing, "I don't care for it."

(That was my first introduction to the great English sickness: open your mouth and you're on trial, judged and sentenced all in the space of two minutes. Oh, the relief of being judged only a foreigner!)

Perhaps it was the second fact that tipped the scales, though. One Sunday morning I found myself sitting in the Methodist church pew with father, Doreen and for some reason, Jack. Just that very morning they had replaced the usual minister, up there in the pulpit, with a substitute – a woman. She appeared from the side door, climbed up the little steps and stood facing us. There was a special hush, unexpected as it was for everybody, then her voice rang out with the first reading of the Bible, and we listened, probably even more closely than usual. Suddenly, Jack stood up and walked out. Two minutes passed and out of the corner of my eye I saw Doreen stand up and go out too. This was worrying. Stealthily, I peered sideways at father, who was looking straight ahead, seemingly intent on the sermon. *Now if you go too, I'm going to be left all alone here!*

Soon after that, Jack's visits ceased and Doreen became, in my eyes, the incarnation of all those songs about lost love, lonesome nights, can't-get-over you. After a year or so, a tall, lanky man brought her home from the dance, charmed mother with his humour and his common sense, and became visiting husband number two. Wouldn't you know it, he was a Catholic too, but she didn't make the mistake of hauling him off to church, except on *The Day*.

Ida's *Day* passed as such days are meant to do, with black and white figures at the altar, photographs in the church doorway and the long table of people laughing and drinking and feeling awkward in their best new clothes. Photographs are what remain; they say *Look, how happy we were!* That is always what we want them to say when we press that button on a scene and we usually succeed in remembering it so, but just occasionally a photograph will tell the whole truth in spite of us. In front of the church they stand, the happy couple in the middle flanked by the two sister bridesmaids; to the left the groom's family, buxom mother, little wizened father and a sister in a new straw hat; to the right, the bride's family, mother, grandmother, father and brother, but you have to look closely otherwise Ken does not appear to be there at all. He is standing behind his father, almost completely concealed.

Doreen's *Day*, just a few years later, followed the same formula but by then I considered myself too old to be dressing up in flounces and bows, so I left the bridesmaiding to the little girls on the groom's side, and was allowed to buy myself a *suit,* which entailed a major expedition to department stores in the city centre. Smart but serviceable was the requirement: something I could wear afterwards, or at least a part of it, the skirt or the jacket. The excitement that all purchases of clothes for special occasions stirs up in any but the most wealthy of people was always diluted down, bubbles quashed, by this indispensable element of *common sense*: dark colours because they save on dry-cleaning bills, plain patterns because they go with everything and suit everywhere. Whims and fancies had no place in the selection.

A New Coat, for example, was a special event, not something to be taken lightly, and it only happened every three or four years. Other things like blouses or skirts were bought casually, but - a New Coat! It had to be planned in advance like a great expedition: on such-and-such a Saturday we will go into Town and get your New Coat. You'll have to get up early. Money was taken out of the bank for this very purpose. The day dawned and off we went, mother and I, the wad of notes in her purse. Even being in town was different, because we went into shops and departments where we didn't normally go, where it was quiet and our wet shoes tip-toed across the thick carpet; or even into small sober-windowed shops that we usually passed by without a glance, where the assistants wore black dresses and lots of face powder and participated in the trying-on process with remarks about turning-up, growing into, wearing well. Eventually, in one of these shops or in one of the big department stores, my New Coat would be wrapped, with the reverence due to it, in rustling white paper and a thick brown bag with string handles (a bag that would not be thrown away later but used to put other things in) and the money was paid, the notes counted out carefully with mother rubbing the corners to make sure there were not two stuck together, and the small change was scraped up.

My heart beat fast to see all these notes being handed over for me - for my New Coat. I felt the weight of responsibility, which would become blame if I didn't like it after all, if I decided when I got home and put it on in my bedroom, that it was horrid and wrong. I had to choose well, I had to be sure, there was no room for error. It was a solemn occasion. That's why, even now when my hair is grey and I can buy, if I should wish to do so, a new coat every year, when I buy one from necessity my heart pounds just a little and I carry away my purchase with a feeling of high daring.

So for my sister's wedding I was a *guest* like the others and in my dark green woollen suit and pink sweater I sat at the table opposite my brother, as awkward and befuddled as he was among the unfamiliar glasses and cutlery, but determined not to show it. The speeches had been made and around us the lunch was settling into the stage where people feel more relaxed, laughing in little clusters, leaning on the table or lounging back in their seats. We sat in our individual solitudes, my brother and I, waiting to be able to go home and become ourselves once again. Looking at him opposite me I knew that he was but a mirror of my own embarrassment, that we were similar in our loneliness, and I disliked him for that and would not help him by talking to him.

He looked across at my face and said, "You've got blackheads on your nose."

The front garden was smaller than the back one but had 'more' in it, so to speak, in the way that English front gardens are kept for being looked at rather than occupied. The grass square was surrounded by a low privet hedge and planted with a couple of rose bushes, and on either side of the porch there were what I always thought of as our pride-and-joy: two large bushes cut into cylindrical shapes. The whole was, of course, maintained impeccably shipshape by father's shears and mower.

When roses are abandoned they do not die right away but run riot, as if the strangling creeping weeds about their throats only spur them on to further efforts. Hedges throw out metre-long shoots in random fashion; dead leaves accumulate underfoot; grass reaches out to its other half across the path. Getting out of a taxi, shortly before my fortieth year,

I saw how grey the curtains looked, how the windows had no shine to them any more and all the paint was peeling away. Had so much time passed since I last walked up this path and lifted the heavy iron knocker?

The curtain in the front room twitched and after a while mother opened the door, but only about two inches. Before her eyes met mine they checked all around me and down the path, and she said nothing. Then she looked at me and opened the door, just enough for me to get inside. Anxiety filled the narrow hallway like some stuffy gas, making it hard to breathe properly. How hollow her cheeks had become... she's old, the thought shocked me, my cheek brushing hers, my mother is an old lady now. Every woman's relationship with her mother is divided into two phases and the line that makes the difference is the moment when you acknowledge that your mother is not only your mother but a person who was a little girl and a young woman before you were ever remotely imagined – who had a life of her own with her pleasures and fears and her dreams that very likely did not come true.

Now that I've come up the path once more, let me pause here on the doorstep a moment, before going in to her, and consider her pleasures. When she wasn't being our mother and his wife, what did she like? How had she been able to remember what she liked, with four children to deal with and an apron tied around her middle from morning till night?

She liked fluffy toys, soft animals, the cat looking up at her. When he died she cried all the afternoon.

She liked reading the flowery obituaries in the evening paper, sometimes reading them out to us. ("Isn't that nice?")

She liked singing. She used to be in the choir as a girl, and always sang her heart out in church.

She liked chocolates. He would occasionally bring home a box of Black Magic and lay it on the arm of her chair when she was out of the room and wait for the pleasure of her to say "Oooh, who's put those there? How nice!" Lovers' tricks for middle-aged people.

She liked colour. No pastel tones for mother.

She liked jokes, reading out loud the best ones from her weekly woman's magazine and laughing, whether we did or not.

She liked men too. She had crushes on film stars, just like a girl. She noticed how the roadworkers, in the summer, looked fit and brown and strong. Fine figures of men, she called them.

She even liked gypsies. They sat on the porch and she gave them cups of tea, to the infinite indignation of Ida. What will people think of us!

She liked children. When I was still at primary school she read something in her magazine about support for African orphans and before you knew it she was writing to two of them, brother and sister, and roped me in to send my own little letters.

She liked life, and people. Look at that Mrs. Evans across the way, cleaning the windows every day! I'd rather be out and about and see a bit of life!

Until you are well into this second phase, you will not really understand your mother, nor will you forgive her.

The first thing I saw in the living room was a pair of wet, navy-blue socks hanging on the back of a chair in front of the fire. An unfamiliar smell of cigarettes led to an ashtray with three stubs in it, laid in the hearth. Mother was nervous, she didn't seem to know where to put herself, her hands were busy all the time.

"He's been here," she said, and I knew she meant Ken. "I've been out. He's still got a key…"

She was afraid. I stood and tried to fit that into some manageable understanding of what was going on. She was afraid of her own son.

"Let's have some tea, shall we?" I suggested.

But in the kitchen it was worse. There were two dirty plates and forks in the sink, takeaway packs in the rubbish bin. The sight of these seemed to throw a switch in her mind and, tea forgotten and me with it, she began to wash up furiously, banging and splashing and muttering darkly to herself. No sooner had I put the kettle on than she had abandoned the dishes and was back in the living room, plugging in the vacuum cleaner and pushing it madly to and fro across the rug. I did not know what to do. She seemed to neither see nor hear me and I watched the violent emotions flicking across her red face until I could bear it no longer and I made her stop and put my arms around her. She slumped against me, unresistant but ungiving, her arms fallen by her sides, and raised her face to heaven.

"*I don't want him here!*"

This cry, the power of it, filled me with terror, and I left her and went outside into the street with the vague idea of calling for an ambulance from a neighbour's house, but really I was losing the situation and I stood there for a second or two at the end of the path, uncertain what to do while I heard her wild voice going on behind me, and then - oh, joyous moment! - there was Ida walking towards me along the street, paying an afternoon visit right at that moment. Her entry in the house was like a wind that blows away dead leaves. After I'd explained, she marched through the hall into the kitchen, where mother was yelling at the sink, and took her by the arm.

"What's all this, Mummy?" Although she seemed to be the mummy just then. "What's going on? I can't have you like this!" Her matter-of-fact tone woke mother from her madness and woke me from my nightmare, and soon we were sitting with cups of tea around the fire.

I never ceased to think how odd it was, that cry; after all, she had never wanted any of us as much as she wanted him.

THE FRONT BEDROOM

Here I parted company with my mother for the first time and entered the world in a great hurry, so that when the midwife arrived there was nothing much left for her to do; mother had done this three times already. When she knew there would be a fourth time, just as she had got them all up and running off to school – one even off to work! – she wasn't too pleased and didn't speak to father for a week. Taking her into a quiet corner, her own mother made her promise not to 'do anything', thereby helping me over the first hurdle so that I could come bawling into the front bedroom of life.

"She'll be a little consolation to you when all the others are gone," was my grandmother's unwise prediction.

The house was full when I came into the world, so I had to sleep in a corner of my parents' bedroom. Space in those terraced houses was a limited commodity and stuffy and dusty was this room, day and night. Pieces of carpet overlapped, leaving a border of linoleum all around that had to be wiped once a week with a cloth. Most of the room was taken up by their double bed with its lumpy mattress, and the wardrobe and a cupboard, for some unfathomable reason called a 'tallboy', stood like things that had been slid in against the wall as afterthoughts. The dressing table stood, as such things usually did, in front of the window, blocking out what little light there was and making it a room always in semi-darkness, even at midday. Rarely were the windows opened and then only a fraction, using the iron arm with the holes in it that fitted over an iron stud in the frame. There were not enough days of a type for flinging windows wide, so they were not made for doing so.

There was one hot, still summer afternoon, when I was about eight or nine, on which I did remove the iron arm from its stud and push open the window. Where was everybody? The street was deserted, sharp shadows slanted across the house fronts. Not a breath of wind, not a footstep broke the silence. There were few cars around then - even on an ordinary grey day you might stand at the window for hours before one went by, and ours was a residential street. I lifted the black iron arm until it was vertical against the pane and then let it fall free. TUMMM, tumtumm, tumtumm, tumumum umumm… it bounced and vibrated several times before coming to rest, the sound filling up the entire street, it seemed to me. TUMMM, tumtumm…. hypnotised by the movement and the fact of being able to let it drop without any damage being done, I went on and on doing it.

"Someone will come," I thought, "Someone will open a window or come upstairs and shout at me to stop." But nobody came, nothing moved, the warm iron fell and the shadows lengthened.

My earliest memory is a sound in the darkness.

I awoke to the frightening loneliness of the very small. What was that? If I had been old enough to formulate a thought in words I would have said, "My father is killing my mother".

In my infant mind and ears the thumping was my father punching my mother and the gasping was the effort it was costing him. The moaning was my mother lying helpless beneath the blows. I did the only thing I could do. I cried, loudly and desperately. There was the sound of a deflating balloon and then my mother's normal voice (oh, joy!) saying quietly, "Stop it, she thinks you're hurting me." Then, more loudly, to me, "It's all right lovey. Go back to sleep." And the darkness took me back into it again.

Shortly after that, the big bed was moved into the back bedroom, where it replaced one of two single beds which, in its turn, was moved into the front bedroom. Another small bed was purchased and this meant that there were now three single beds in the front bedroom. My two sisters shared the second room and my brother had the smallest room to himself until I took it over after his marriage, when he was twenty-one and I was eleven.

In my third year I spent many weeks lying in bed, so close to ending my short existence that my mother sat on the doorstep and cried with her neighbour. I was aware only of two things: the regular apparition of big people at my bedside, bending over me and saying cheery things to me, and the strange gentleness and kindness of my mother bending over me with troubled eyes. My infant illness brought comfort, soft words and the bringing of gifts, and above all the gentle touch of her hand, no longer pulling or pushing. Was that why it took me so long to get better?

The elderly doctor was replaced by his younger partner. Enthusiastic and modern, he tried a new drug on me, saying this would have me up and about in no time. I lay in my bed one afternoon gazing at the light coming through the light brown curtains, which had a large pattern of squares with black vertical marks inside them. As I gazed, the black marks became human figures and began to move. I made them walk from one square into another, and it seemed to me, as I lay there on my side staring, that some picture story was being told like in a comic strip, and that I was, at the same time, telling it and reading it. The side-effects of the new drug became apparent to others when I started screaming that my bed and the ceiling were covered with black insects. Forty years after that, I came across an article in a newspaper that mentioned an experimental drug which had been tried out on children in the UK in the Fifties, and hurriedly withdrawn, which contained LSD.

But when, from the same bedroom window, I saw the UFO, that was not an hallucination. In my memory, I am alone, so it must have been in the few hours after my bedtime and before they came to bed. There are no shutters on English houses, lamplight and the moon can shine through the curtains into your sleep and wake you up. I named the silvery-edged shapes to myself one by one: wardrobe, mirror, chair… all strangers now in the light that had woken me shining on my face. I awoke, slipped out from beneath the heavy blankets that shielded me from the icy cold, and took the two steps between my bed and the window. Here, my bare feet on the linoleum border, I moved the curtain aside with a finger.

All the street was in darkness, not a single window lit and all the streetlamps out. The rooftops, punctuated by chimney blocks, divided the dark from the darker, and in the upper darkness a single globe hung over it all, glittering. Its light was clear, cold and self-contained, it did not illuminate the sky like a full moon does, but it had woken me like a torch pointed at my window. The surface of it seemed to be pitted like a golf ball, but there was no movement at all. It simply hung there above the silent, sleeping world. Over to my right, lower down and looking, by comparison, small and sickly, was the moon. The stars twinkled in the wintry night and there was a great silence all around. I waited. Something will happen, I thought, if I thought at all, so cold was the room around me. Slowly, the moon slid away round the side of the house but the glittering sphere stayed steady and bright.

Cold I was, cold and sleepy, and when I could no longer feel my feet or keep my eyes open, I slipped back into bed and fell asleep immediately. It had never entered my head to go and call someone, nor did I say anything the next morning. *They will say I was dreaming, they won't believe me.* Not even when Ken came home from work and told us that some of his mates had seen something, not even then did I share it.

They will say I was dreaming.

Sometimes I was, and sometimes I wasn't, that was the trouble.

Men had striped pyjamas in those days, blue and white striped cotton, with a drawstring waist on the trousers. His smile was the thing that scared me – at that moment, in the dim light of the bedroom, it was not there for fun or affection, it was there to distract me from his large hand which covered mine and compelled it to remain where he wanted it, while he spoke soothingly, with a little quivering laugh, attempting to persuade me that it was as nice for me as it was for him. Then a fluster, breathless, with a handkerchief and whispered reassurance.

Was that a dream, that broke to the surface only after decades of life and the first grey hairs? Or is it a memory, like the memory of when I awoke in the dark to the strangest sound, impossible to identify at first: father crying. I peeked through half-open lids and saw him, in the shadowy room, sitting up in his bed with his hands over his face, weeping in that dry, jerky way men have. (Where was she? Was that the time she spent some days in hospital with a prolapse?) Words were jerked out between the sobs.

"Oh God, help me… oh please God… help me… I've tried my best… please God!"

I didn't know what he was pleading about. Perhaps it was the trouble with my brother, perhaps there wasn't enough money, perhaps it was my mother's illness. Perhaps it was the very same night of his strange smile.

Father crying. How could that be? Father knew everything, there was never any use asking mother, she would say ask your father, he'll explain, he'll know: check the timetable, book the tickets, pay the bills, sort Right from Wrong. Standards, said Father, there are Standards. Father! What tall pillars were constructed with those six letters, the temple where one mounted the steep steps in cotton ankle socks to stand at the imposing door and ask with upturned face for wisdom! Afraid to move, hardly daring to breathe, I listened to the pillars cracking and crumbling, the temple falling and I knew, for the first time, that there was no protection, that I was alone in the world and would have to fend for myself.

Bedrooms were for sleeping and for being ill, they didn't have tables, so any homework I had to do at the dining table after tea, but this wasn't difficult because there was no television until I was nine. Bedrooms were for secrets.

Ken was coming out of short trousers into long ones and

he secretly smoked. He knew that I kept in the bedroom a Dr. Barnardo's box in the form of a house with a slot in the roof and a plastic plug underneath, to collect money for the orphans. Ken crept in to my bedside when nobody else was upstairs and whispered urgently, "Lend us ninepence for five Woodies."

The light from the landing was glowing softly behind the open door. He was jumpy, looking over his shoulder.

"I can't".

"I'll give it you back, honest".

God sees you, said father, wherever you are, whatever you're doing. And - HE KNOWS WHAT YOU'RE THINKING.

The clouds parted and a great eye glared down on the town, on the street, on me under the blankets in a corner of the room.

"No, I can't."

"Go on…"

"No."

My brother's eye glared down on me, and it was worse than the eye of God, because it meant he hated me.

"*Mean thing!*"

I first became fully aware of Ken in my life one summer, on holiday, there on the rocks, the never-ending white rocks with the dark places between that were frightening because there was no knowing how far the darkness went or what might suddenly come scrambling out of it over feet or, in my case, fingers, because I was too small to walk on the rocks, I had to clamber. Steps led down from the promenade, not to the sand but to this immense stretch of white boulders, the town's defence against the fierce winter seas. Beyond the boulders there were smaller rocks, and beyond those, smooth white pebbles that knew the sea well, and then at last the flat golden sand, the heavy castle sand that slid so satisfyingly compact out of the bucket. Under my feet in their unaccustomed, summer-holiday blue sandals, spiders occasionally dashed from one cave to another, horrifying me when they came near my fingers. When I stopped and looked up, squinting in the strong light, I could see the faraway line of white waves – the astonishing Atlantic Ocean, up to your neck one minute, waving at you from the horizon the next – the figures of children paddling, even their excited voices arriving on the breeze, mingling with the seagulls' screams, and it seemed as if I would never make it safely to join them, but remain stranded there forever on the hot white rocks, unable to go on or go back.

A pair of dusty brown shoes were planted firmly beside my hands on the rock and Ken, in his first long trousers, held out his hand to me. His shadow fell across me as I looked up at his white shirt, his hair falling over his forehead and the Superman comic rolled up in his other hand.

"Come on, I'll take you."

"I can do it."

But he kept his hand there anyway, measuring his pace to mine, and when eventually I had to take it, quietly without looking up, he didn't say anything. We went on over the rocks together, the sun beating down on us, and so it was, through our linked hands, that I became aware of him in my world and me in his. Ken knew things. He showed me how to make a sixpence spin for ages and how to make it stick on your forehead. He showed me a dirty trick to make it look as if you were shoving your finger right up your nose to the knuckle. He drew eyes on his fist and there was a big, toothless mouth laughing at me. He mended things, like the handle on my bucket and the wounded, wide-eyed doll whose arm came away in my hand and lay there like an uncooked sausage.

"Give it here, I'll fix it for you."

He pulled the elastic out of the armhole and twisted it back onto the shoulder stump, showing me the mysterious empty innards of my doll.

"Watch this…"

"Take a card…"

"Close your eyes…"

Tricks and jokes and sleight of hand, comic-book magic, winning my heart. But it came to an end. I hovered around on the back step as he crouched over a tin.

"What's them?"

"Maggots."

"What they for?"

"Catch the fish."

"Can I come?"

"No."

"Why not?"

"No."

"Ah, go on!"

"NO!"

He would have been a laughing stock. Kid sister with you?

He left me then, or I left him, after the visit to the opticians, my first pink NH glasses and the discovery of the Word. After I got the world in focus, every opening of a book was another great heavy door of the world opening on its massive hinges, letting in the light and a glimpse of infinite green garden. White paths led away invitingly in all directions and water trickled and danced somewhere, unseen but promising much to the thirsty. Full of excitement, I ran - an effortless springing of limbs, like flying - down the paths, not waving, not looking back, until a very long time had passed and then, when I did pause, raised my eyes from the pages and turned, I was astonished to find that Ken was a small speck in the distance. I longed for him to come with me, but he would not, could not.

"Do you know, Ken didn't speak until he was three."

One quiet sunny afternoon, sitting together over cups of tea in the single-bed apartment of her old age, mother handed me this historical fact along with the biscuits, but something in her tone made it clear to me that she knew its importance and that, at the same time, she could not have said exactly what it meant.

Brain imaging studies have shown significant differences between the brain activity of people stammering as compared with fluent speakers.

"The doctor said – I do remember it – he said 'This little boy is going to need a lot of love'. That's what he said."

Stammering is characterised by stoppages and disruptions in fluency which interrupt the smooth flow and timing of speech. Speech may sound forced, tense or jerky.

Everyone turned and looked when it was his turn to read out loud and the teacher was always impatient.

"The *what*, boy? Speak up!"

"The b-b-b-ba…"

"The *battle*, boy, the *battle*! Of what?"

"The b-b-battle of W-w-w…"

The battle of the Word.

People who stammer may avoid certain words or situations which they know will cause them difficulty. Stammering is not simply a speech difficulty but a serious communication problem. For the child or adult who stammers it can undermine their confidence and self-esteem, and affect their interactions with others as well as their education and employment prospects.

The Word was his enemy, and he twisted his face into a sneer if he found one of my schoolbooks left on the chair where he wanted to sit:

"Is this *your stuff*?"

After his marriage, when I took over Ken's bedroom, I hardly ever went into the front bedroom any more, unless it was to fetch mother something from the 'tallboy'. Twenty years later I had occasion to enter it two more times.

The first time was during a warm summer night, not very late but already dark, after the long northern twilight that I came to miss when I no longer had it. Mother had already gone upstairs to get ready for bed, while downstairs father was pottering about doing those little things people do before they call it a day. I was washing and putting away the few cups left from our tea, and you might have thought that in such circumstances there was an air of tranquillity and end-of-day satisfaction, with just a few murmured exchanges to confirm the human relationships. Nothing of the sort. The atmosphere was charged with anxiety and sorrow. It was my second day of another flying visit and I couldn't wait to leave again. Ken was not, himself, in the house, yet his presence was in every word and gesture they made, and even hovered in the silences. By then his life was spiralling downwards at frightening speed – no more jobs, no more marriage, kids lost to him, and worse, although nobody ever said it to me but I knew, because I saw the syringe behind the curtain and she refused to look at it; said she knew nothing about it. He was falling fast and having to watch him was wearing her out, breaking her heart. She was beginning to turn on her husband because she had some incoherent idea that he *could* do something, but that he *would not*.

While I was there, each of them tried to pull me to their side in small, subtle ways, which would have gone unnoticed by an outsider, but which were giving me a sensation of being torn apart. I had to go.

The kitchen settled, I called goodnight to father, who was fixing the window latches in the living room, and went upstairs. On the landing, I heard a small sound like a very tiny kitten mewing, coming from behind the front bedroom door. I went to push it open, but it would not move very far because mother was lying in a heap behind it. I had to push my way in, and as I bent down to her I could hear him coming up the stairs. My heart was thumping so, I thought my chest would burst. She was quietly weeping and gasping as I held her to try and get her up, and she managed to say that she had taken all her sleeping pills. Father heard this just as he appeared round the door, and his face crumpled like that of a small child, and in the same role he began to paddle his slippered feet, saying over and over,

"Oh no, oh no, oh no!"

I saw that I was the only adult just then. I am calm in a storm.

"Go to a phone," I said firmly to him. There was still no phone in the house, in the Seventies. He stood there, suddenly helpless.

"She'll be all right, but you *have to go to the neighbours and phone.*"

He fled. Somehow, I managed to wrestle her onto the bed, and I thought, I don't know why, that it would be better to try to keep her awake. I bent over her, saying heaven knows what, waiting for the blessed siren of the ambulance.

"I just wanted to have a long long sleep," she whispered.

The next morning, with a collar on her neck, drinking a cup of tea in the living room, she quietly said, "God will forgive me, won't he?"

The second time I went upstairs was about ten years later. By then, I no longer stayed with them when I visited, but with Doreen and her family, and she and I went together to see them.

"He's in bed," said mother as we crowded into the living room together, and in her tone the disapproval of this was clear. Upstairs, in the fusty closed room with dirty windows and faded carpets, he lay propped on three pillows - he always had three, he said it helped against his asthma - apparently slowly starving to death, in grey sheets. She took him a sandwich now and then, but she could not, or would not, help him to keep clean or to take his pills, and how can a person who's losing his memory know which pill to take when? The doctor would come as part of his rounds, deeply harassed and always in a hurry, and reel off his litany: "The white one and the blue one in the morning, the long one after lunch, another white one before sleeping..." and who would remember that after he had gone?

My father's skin was grey and cold; we managed to get his filthy pyjama jacket off and Doreen held it up to me like the damning evidence of a wife's criminal neglect. Mother remained downstairs, out of reach of our wrath. I brought some warm water in a bowl and with a flannel washed his hands and face, and he submitted like a child. The room was sour with smells of dust and urine. Doreen went out and bought a tin of soup, heated it up and we watched as he wolfed it down gratefully. Suddenly he paused, with the spoon in mid-air, and said, "Oooh", with a shiver, "Did you feel that?"

"What?"

"Oooh, that wave of cold air, just now… freezing."

There were no windows open and it was August. That he was losing his reason became clear in stages; on a previous visit, I had found food secreted in places where it had no business to be, growing blue, probably hidden there from her; he began to leave his speech unfinished:

"I've to go to the…."

"To where, Dad?"

"To the…. oh… I just have to go…"

"Don't worry about it."

"To the… oh, what is it?... I have to…"

And the dreadful struggle always ended in defeated silence.

Now, he leaned back on his pillows while we fussed around the room doing what it was possible to do, and he said, "I can't believe I'm eighty-nine."

My blood ran cold.

"You're not eighty-nine, Dad, you're seventy-six."

I was still staying with Doreen when the news arrived that mother had had no option but to call an ambulance, because he came downstairs and asked her where his wife was, and got annoyed because he knew she was there somewhere. That was his last day at home, and the first night that mother slept in the front bedroom alone.

THE BACK BEDROOM

When mother or father used the phrase *the girls*, they meant Doreen and Ida. I was too young to be included in it. There were *the girls*, there was *our Ken* and then *the little 'un,* which was me. Destined always to be the *little 'un*, I hated, at twelve or thirteen, to be presented by Doreen, at the shops or in the church, as *my kid sister*.

We hardly ever bumped into each other, the girls and me; they were at work and I was at school during the day. In the evening, dancing took them out in their heels and wide skirts with black waspie belts. By the time father had enough money to have a summer holiday again, they took theirs with friends. To me, they were always women, and I lived among a flurry of outspoken, laughing, powerful women in bright floral prints and the waft of talcum powder, while the men were shadowy, quiet figures, gloomy even, that came and went in the background, slipping into their places with the least disturbance. Even their clothes seemed to say *we are only the accompaniment*: blacks, greys, dark browns, white or pale blue shirts.

On Saturdays the women dealt with dirt and dust and the men were scattered like rats, to go where they would, but out of the way. Doreen might get the bathroom and Ida the beds, or the hoovering, while mother reigned in the minuscule kitchen, a place for a solitary monarch. Thus they practised for their own houses, where they were to have gadgets which, for the time being, were not available. I was not considered too small to participate, and into my small hand a yellow duster was crushed and I was shown the right way to use it on wooden chair backs and legs, a training which did not 'take' very well as I have always tried to avoid it ever since. I prefer to remember mother's words of one particular day:

"Never mind – the dust'll be there when I'm gone. I'd rather be out and about."

So we were not dirty, but we were not shiny squeaky clean like in the adverts, which mother always saw through. ("Oh yes, as if you could get it clean with one swipe like that!")

Doreen and Ida shared a bedroom all through their adolescence and most of their twenties, until they married. I have never shared a bedroom except in hotels, but I can imagine the difficulties, or the comforts, of such an arrangement, especially in such a small room. The room with the most light, it looked out onto the back garden, the opposite houses and between them, the main road, and when the sun came in with its natural warmth it was sometimes too hot, because this was the room that contained the boiler.

The section of the main road that could be seen from the window sometimes kept me standing alone at the window-sill, counting the cars that passed. There wasn't an endless stream in those years – one would go past and I could count up to ten before the next one appeared. We went everywhere by bus, and when somebody went out to catch one, if I waited at the window for five minutes I could see them in that section visible between the houses, walking to the bus stop, a small distant figure that belonged to me, but had taken on a strange 'otherness' by being out there.

The light blue flowered wallpaper surrounded two single beds, one behind the door, the other against the opposite wall with only about three paces between them, and a large chest of drawers. *For your bottom drawer,* mother used to say to one of them when they received a household-type present. For years I didn't understand that this meant a stock of things that would be useful when they got married, what was once called a *trousseau*. Once, when I was alone, I even pulled open the bottom drawer, thinking to find something secret and special in there, and was disappointed to find only boring white folded things, like in any other drawers.

In one corner of the room there was the airing cupboard, which contained the boiler and some wooden shelves where the washing was laid after partially drying outside. But the best thing by far in this room was the dressing-table, with three mirrors that fascinated me when I discovered them. By carefully positioning them I could see my profile (which I began immediately to hate) and then with a small change of position I could see myself in an endless succession of reflections that got smaller and smaller, like two tunnels running off to left and right.

I only ever went into this room when there was nobody around. This was the room of the women, it always smelt of perfume, hair lacquer and that elusive, tepid odour of females in their dens; here I could get glimpses of the future feminine world that I was destined for. Lipsticks could be tried out and then washed off hastily in the bathroom, and the 'waspie' belts of black elastic could be played with before being fastened around my waist to grip my childish fat and block my breath. Necklaces and lockets fastened round my neck were examined for effect in the mirror and I tried the high-heeled shoes on, but they failed to attract me, even then as now. I opened the jars and tubes and sniffed at them, and sprayed myself with perfume from a small bottle with a rubber ball attached to it. Mascara was a messy thing which I soon lost interest in because it made vertical black smudges on the lenses of my glasses. I examined the plastic hair rollers with strands of hair tangled in them, and the dish full of brown hair clips with little bulbous ends that you could pull off. There was so much involved in being a grown-up woman, so many little things you had to have and use, at once exciting and tedious. Once I took a pillow from the bed and pushed it up my skirt to see what I looked like with 'a bun in the oven'. I was the only one not to have seen mother with a bun in the oven.

If the dressing-table was a place to try on identities, the wardrobe mirror was pure Alice. I stood before the wardrobe and explored the strange mirror-world, where my right hand was my left hand, where I could never see myself as I really was: familiar, yet not quite right, an eyebrow with a different curve and my hair parted on the other side. All I could see of the wardrobe was the brass handle dangling in front of the glass.

"Oh Kitty! How nice it would be if we could only get through into Looking Glass House! I'm sure it's got oh such beautiful things in it! Let's pretend there's a way of getting through into it somehow, Kitty. Let's pretend the glass has got all soft, like gauze, so that we can get through. Why, it's turning into a sort of mist now, I declare! It'll be easy enough to get through…" She was up on the chimney-piece while she said this, though she hardly knew how she had got there. And certainly the glass was beginning to melt away, just like a bright silvery mist…"

The cold glass lay against my cheek like a firm hand devoid of compassion. No amount of pretending would melt it, would get me out of there into somewhere else.

In this room, Ida dressed for her wedding, the three-mirrored dressing-table in full use. In this room Doreen lay and wept when she lost her boyfriend, the one who could not cope with female preachers.

In this room, many years later when Ida and Doreen were in their own homes and I was in my last years at school, flexing my wings to fly the nest, I came one day, at four in the afternoon, to wake up my brother.

I knew, from mother's letters, why he was there. An early marriage founded on an unwanted pregnancy rarely lasts the course, and this one lasted barely a year. After the birth of the baby, I had been with mother to see them at their rented home: a tiny terraced house in a poky street whose name boded no good - *Craven* Street. It was dark and cramped inside and seemed dusty; a few sticks of second-hand furniture bearing the rubbed marks of other people's lives; grubby little mats and naked light bulbs; the young girl who was nervous because mother was looking round; the huge pram - the only shiny thing - taking up the narrow hallway.

"Let's have some tea."

It was Ken who said it, the girl didn't seem to know what to do. It was as if she was playing house, as if none of it was real. She gathered cups together. We all stood awkwardly, waiting for her to take charge, to be the host, a role far beyond her capabilities.

"Isn't there anything to eat?"

Ken seemed annoyed with her.

"Have a look in there," she answered, nodding towards the wall.

She spoke as if she didn't know. In the cupboard on the wooden shelves there was nothing but a cruet and a half-empty jar of jam.

"Never mind," said mother, her face saying the opposite.

The baby started crying and the girl stuffed a bottle in its mouth. Its blanket seemed grubby and I did not want to hold it. They talked, on and off, and I looked around and saw how different it was from our house, and I knew how sad mother was feeling, but I didn't yet know the depth of sadness that my brother had fallen into.

Two months went by. Once or twice they came on a Sunday afternoon, she in her best coat, the baby girl wrapped up in a blanket and carried on the bus. Everybody tried their best, as if this situation was no different from a visit by my sisters and their husbands, but despite the time-honoured rituals of tea and cakes and domestic chatter, it was different: beneath and behind it all was a deep dissatisfaction, an unnameable awareness of it being all wrong from the start. Some people say that babies have invisible antennae, supersensitive feelers that capture the slightest shift in atmosphere even before they begin to capture words. We may know when we have not been wanted.

Within three months, the baby girl died. The cause of death was laid down as yet another inexplicable cot death. There was the signed certificate. Let it rest. However it was, the baby, the whole rhyme and reason of their hasty marriage, was gone.

Barely a year went by and then he came back to mother by himself one day, filling an ashtray with stubs and calling his wife a 'whore'; the theatrical word sat strangely on his tongue. He had been working nights, to earn more, and came home earlier one morning. The man fled out through the back door, half-naked. He sat with his rage and humiliation by the fireside and mother plied him with tea and all her attention while she silently rejoiced in having known it all beforehand.

Living in my schoolwork and my school uniform in those days, I did not really know how or where my brother was living; occasionally he would be there, in the corner of the living-room couch, flicking ash into the hearth and staring mutely at the television. Then he might vanish from the house for weeks on end and nobody knew where he slept. When he appeared in the middle of the day sometimes it became apparent that he had lost his job, and the heydays of jobs for the asking were over. From my sixth-form safe distance, which had me going home each evening as if I were being sent momentarily into exile from my real home, echoes reached me from a world as yet unknown to me: *dole, divorce, social services, court*s, and mother and father quarrelled in a way I had never known them to do. If Doreen or Ida happened to be present, they put their oars in too, but nobody seemed ever to reach a conclusion. Sometimes they even argued with one another about him over Ken's head, while he sat in silence as if they weren't there at all, as if he were quite alone in the room. Then when they had done he would get up, light another cigarette and walk out without saying a word.

Only once, there in his usual place by the hearth, did he

say something that was on his mind. Still young, still reasonably healthy, he had begun to hear the clock ticking away and nothing, nothing safe yet, nothing achieved.

"Ah, no," he said, in answer to some encouraging words from mother, "*a man's finished by the time he's forty*."

Meanwhile, I had flown the nest and was living far away in my first student year. When I went home for Christmas, Easter or summer visits, sometimes he was there, sometimes he was not. This time, I found he had been there for several days, and when I arrived he was taking a nap upstairs in the empty back bedroom, now stripped of its female aura and simply a room for storing awkward things and for anyone to sleep in.

"Poor lad", mother said, "I think he's not slept properly. I've to wake him up at four he says, to go somewhere…"

"I'll do it".

Why did I say that? As I mounted the stairs I was strangely anxious. We had not met for years. Who was this man that lay on his belly in the bed, clutching the pillow in his arms, so deep in the safety of his sleep that he didn't know I was standing at the door watching him? *I should have gently called him to the surface and when he was conscious I should have sat down and asked him to tell me the roots of his sorrow. We were no longer children, he would have confided in me and together we would have found a way for him to come out of the depths, to go on living and be all that he could have been…* A fine fantasy. Life is not what happens in films, people don't talk like that, don't wait for the others to get through their lines. We don't even know our own lines. I prodded him cruelly with a finger.

"It's four o'clock."

Not many years after that, when he could not be said to have called anywhere home, I entered that room again and looked around its poor abandoned sticks of furniture, in the stale air of unused rooms. By then, mother had given up dusting altogether and a grey film lay on the dressing-table and the chest of drawers. The uncovered mattress displayed its stripes and hollows like a ploughed field. The afternoon was warm and quiet, as it had been so long ago when I thought I could escape through the mirror. I turned to the window, where the view was unchanged except for the wall of a new factory or warehouse that could be seen in the distance between the houses, where once there had been only trees. Out of the corner of my eye I found something glinting on the windowsill, hidden behind the curtain. A syringe. I held it up to her face.

"What's this?"

She frowned and looked away.

"I don't know."

"Well, is it father's? Does he have injections of medicine?"

"No, not that I know of."

"Well" – I wanted to shake her – "how did it *get* there then?!"

"I don't know."

She would not consider the thing.

THE SMALL BEDROOM

Before it was mine, it was his. Just a few metres square, probably never meant to be a proper bedroom but only an 'extra' room for a baby to sleep in, or to store things in, it held precious little: a single bed, a chair and a chest of drawers. There wasn't room for a wardrobe; Ken kept his everyday clothes in a cupboard on the landing, and the special, hang-up-properly clothes that weren't needed very often in the big wardrobe in the front bedroom. This tiny room had a window that looked out onto the street-lamp and beyond, to three tall chimneys you could see between the houses, which mother said were the 'power station' and which gave her the means to say (mysteriously to me) 'it's blowing for rain''. I silently greeted these chimneys every morning throughout my adolescence, until they were replaced, in the window of my first year alone in another town, by three tall poplar trees full of raucous birds.

I never entered this room before it was mine. Ken had his secret private existence in there and the door was always closed. Only mother went in, to clean and to take hot drinks when he lay in bed with a bad cold, which only he was allowed to do without being told not to make a fuss.

One night, I was awakened by movement and sounds upon the landing, voices that were agitated while trying to be quiet. Suddenly mother appeared above me and said crossly, "You'll have to get up and get dressed. Come on, you'll have to come downstairs."

Dozily, I pulled on my school things and stumbled downstairs, where my sister Doreen was walking about in her nightie and people were talking over one another. I fell asleep again in an armchair, but not before someone had said to me, "Your brother's set his room on fire!"

It was more smoke than fire, and there was little for the fire brigade to do when they arrived; smouldering sheets and billows of smoke going out of the window. He had been so terrified of father's reaction that he had tried to put it out himself without telling anyone, and Doreen, on waking, had found him rushing back and forth between his room and the bathroom with cups of water. "Don't tell father!" he pleaded with her, more afraid of him than the fire, but there wasn't much choice. The ceiling had to be whitewashed, there were a few days of cloudy silences and there was no more smoking in bed.

"He never took that much trouble with Ken." Mother

appeared to be talking to herself, or to the piece of stuff she held in her fingers for mending, although the words were uttered in my presence and were meant for me. Father had not only consulted me about what kind of wallpaper he was going to use to redecorate the bedroom for my moving in, but had even taken me with him to choose the paint: two tones of pink and pink flowers on the walls, soon to be lost anyway under posters of Cliff and The Beatles. She was full of resentment - on top of his no longer living at home with us, it seemed to her as if we were trying to cancel all traces of Ken, to say that not only would he never sleep in there again but that he had never slept in there at all. The walls, the paintwork, the curtains, everything was changed, a small cupboard was put up on the wall, there being no room for a bedside table, and a new dressing table was bought which left me with about half a metre of space to stand up in, between it and my bed, when I got up in the morning. It had a long horizontal mirror which neither mother nor I ever cleaned.

"I don't know how you can see your face in that," said Doreen.

So at last this room became mine, for seven years, a place that I could mark with my own life. Now homework could be done sitting on the bed, books could be read propped on the pillow before putting out the light and I was free to examine with trepidation my growing body, in the mirror and not, in the privacy of my very own space.

At the age of eleven, we were still children in those days;

our clothes were not miniature copies of adult women's clothes and our comics offered tales of girls' friendships, animals, occasionally a brightly coloured plastic ring, but no trace of boys. In my brand new, stiff and slightly-too-large (to last) uniform, I took my place among the other grammar school girls who'd been sifted out of the office/factory fodder, and learned very quickly that uniforms do not iron out the differences.

What we called 'games', not sport, were obligatory twice a week. The changing room was crowded, stuffy and always rippling with giggles and girls' chatter. White vests and navy knickers (obligatory uniform, with your name sewn inside) made us seem a flock of gulls jostling for place among the wooden benches. Not having yet made a real friend, I was changing my clothes alone when suddenly I was approached by three girls who were giggling together.

"Hello, *Jean*."

Heehee…

"Hello…"

"What's that brown mark on your back, *Jean*?"

Heeheehee…

There was no wondering about it. Although I had not seen my back I knew instantly what she meant, a new knowledge that illuminated my home life with a merciless white light. The leader came closer and pretended to peer inside my ear.

"Oooh, look here! You could grow potatoes in there!"

Alone in my new bedroom, among fresh paint and bright flowery curtains, I sat on the bed and examined my body: the grey patches around my ankles and behind my knees, the grey streaks in the folds of my elbows and the hard grey skin on the outside. I got up off the bed and wiping a hole with my fingers in the dust of the mirror I examined the grey streaks around my neck. I went to my sisters' bedroom and by using the three mirrors I looked at my back, then I returned to my own room and closed the door again. Sitting there on my bed with my hands around my legs, I gazed in wonder at my grey ankles, fingering them with care, but I was not able, then, to formulate in words what I knew it meant. *Neglect* was not a word of common currency in my growing vocabulary. At a certain point, very early on, having done the essential minimum for me, she left me to myself. I was not told to have a bath, to clean my teeth, to wash my hair, I was not taught how. Nobody knew that, because although there were six of us in such a small house, we never saw the flesh of one another's bodies apart from face and hands, and if we should happen to stumble across someone half-dressed by opening a door at the wrong moment, we looked the other way. Nobody knew, and I had to wait for the world to tell me. When it did, I took home the shame and kept it quietly in my room, where it slowly burned down to ashes as I attempted to take care of my body.

I had few clothes. Most of the time I was in school uniform, which I didn't bother to change even after coming home at four o'clock, merely removing my tie and changing my shoes for slippers. At weekends I wore other things but there was little or no difference between staying-in clothes and going-out clothes. Doreen and Ida, both in their twenties, came home from work, ate and, twice a week, changed into their dancing clothes. Ken, in his late teens, took off his work overalls and put on his suit and tie, combed his hair with Brylcreem and passed a cloth over his shoes before heading out again. I did my homework and watched TV, and it never entered my mind that I might be doing something else in the hours between teatime and bedtime. Boys did not exist yet, nor did I have a close girlfriend until I was sixteen. Life was lived at school or at home, in my books and pictures, which seemed enough to take me off wherever I wanted to be, and my small bedroom was a large part of my life, where I pinned up my heroes, dreamed of being a cowgirl (white horse, white hat), read about Lassie, Black Beauty and the Famous Five, and one day decided that God did not exist. In this room I woke up joyful on Christmas Days, fingering the ice ferns on the windowpane, and on other bad days slammed the world out with a great bang to lie roaring upon my bed of coals.

"What are you doing up there?" mother often called from the foot of the stairs after tea.

"Homework."

"Well, mind that electric fire near the bed and don't be up there all evening."

Why not? Why did she want me down in the living

room? It wasn't as if she wanted to talk to me. We would only sit watching the TV. Sometimes she pushed open the door of my room, holding on to it and peeping round it but not coming in. The door was slightly too long and made a *shuffing* noise as it strained over the carpet. When I heard this sound I looked up from my book like a dog guarding a bone.

"You'll ruin your eyes reading in that light."

"I can see all right."

She would look around the room then, as if searching for something else that might make me stop what I was doing. Books, books, books.

"It's only more stuff to dust", mother used to say when she did the housework, although she never said that of all the little ornaments she collected on windowsills and mantelpiece.

There were no bookcases in any rooms, only a small, two-shelf affair that stood on the upstairs landing just outside my room, packed tightly with a few very old, thick brown-backed volumes which father had inherited from his parents or grandparents. *In His Footsteps, The Universal Encyclopaedia of Useful Information, Journey to the Centre of the Earth, The Illustrated Medical Encyclopaedia.* This last one I consulted with thumping heart when nobody was around; it had special pop-up pictures in layers that enabled you to peel open the human body in stages, taking away the skin, then the raw-meat muscles, then the red and blue arteries and veins, right down to the awful skeleton. The pages of these books were gold-edged and when I pulled one carefully from the shelf it sent up a faint smell which grew stronger on opening the cover, inside of which there were brown spots and yellow stains. *He never reads them*, mother said, they were just there, gathering dust. She hated the shelves even more after my encyclopaedia was added. This was a weekly illustrated magazine entitled *Knowledge* and after reading one issue I had asked father if I could have a subscription, and eventually you could order binders and end up with five volumes.

Mother flicked her duster angrily at the shelves.

When she had finished school at fourteen my mother was sent by her parents to learn "short-hand and typing" so that she could go and work in an office. "Ooh, I *hated* it!" she confessed to me one day, "So that didn't last long. Told them I wasn't going any more." To complete the process of her alienation from books and paper, a 'doctor' told my grandmother that if she let her daughter peer into books too much she would ruin her eyesight.

Father never bought any books, but he was a frequent library goer, especially after his retirement. That he might prefer to take the bus alone to the library rather than another bus to town with mother was a sore point in their later years, which filled her with resentment. When he could no longer recognise his wife and his fragmented self was placed in strangers' hands, one of the first things she did, when she was forced to realise that he was not coming home again, was to gather up those books on the little shelf, all of them, and take them down to the dustbin.

THE BATHROOM

I only realised how small it was when I came home on my first visit after leaving: it seemed to me that I stood high above the washbasin and that there was barely enough room for my hands in it, so tiny it seemed. I shifted my hands between the hot tap and the cold tap and looked at the windowsill in front of me; a fresh-air spray and a spare toilet roll covered by one of mother's crinoline ladies; on the linoleum, a pale blue mat around the toilet base and another mat by the side of the bath, barely two yards between them; the wooden seat of my childhood had been replaced by a white plastic one; above the toilet, a small wall-mounted cabinet with a mirror; next to the door, a plastic bin for the dirty clothes and above that, a one-bar electric fire high up on the wall. Unlike the kitchen, nothing much changed in here. The bath bore the same black mark shaped like New Zealand, where the enamel had worn off, which I had been looking at all my life.

This was the only place where each of six people might be alone for a short time, although there was usually somebody waiting their turn. Now, it occurs to me that perhaps the one who most appreciated that solitude was mother.

She must have been very tired, on that evening when I would not keep still in the bath, inside my two or three-year-old skin, and she shook me hard so that I slipped under the water. I was very small, and it seemed like a swimming pool. As it closed over my face I heard her saying, "Yes, go on, go under, then I won't have the bother of you any more!" at the same time pulling me up to safety with a strong hand around my wrist. Fear washed about in my mouth and the small heart was pierced. She tried to make amends, comforting and towelling and denying her meaning, but it was done, could not be undone.

I have had to live most of my life before understanding her, as she was then, a middle-aged woman with three children already, two at school and one even at work, who was suddenly told that it was all to do over again, one more time, nappies and bottles and all the baby clothes and cot thrown out long ago, not even a pram to use. First I reached an understanding with my mind; it took longer for the heart. When she needed a kind word, a comforting hug, in her later years, I sat still on her sofa and gave her nothing. "What's the matter?" I said, because she was staring at me. Her sofa was one of the few things that she had been allowed to take with her into the residential home - living room, kitchen and bedroom - where she spent her last few years, torn unceremoniously from the house she had presided over for fifty years. But that can't have broken her heart, because that was already so battered and patched up that there can't have been anything it couldn't withstand; not even my indifference. She was staring at me in a lull in the conversation: this odd daughter of mine, appearing now and then from God-knows-where, tanned and looking ever more like her father, not wanting for her life any of the things I wanted. Who is she? That's what I used to think she was thinking.

"Nothing," she said. "I'm just thinking how nice you are and how much I love you."

She might have hit me over the head with a shovel. Thirty years too late, mother, thirty years too late! No, I did not get up and hug her and say I loved her too. I sat there, stunned, as stunned as the child wrapped in a towel after her bath. I have never been able to swim, despite having been to some of the loveliest beaches, despite my lifelong wish to live by the sea.

I used to examine the traces of other people that I found in the bathroom - knowledge of them that could not be found elsewhere. In the wall cabinet lived a shaving brush - I felt its soft creamy bristles and fluffed it over my face. The razor was heavy in my fingers and I dared not experiment with it. Now and then, my sisters' underwear appeared hanging on a line, dripping, over the bath: elastic girdles with metal suspenders, bras and fine nylon stockings with seams up the back.

"Oh, she's been wringing her stockings in the towels again!" was mother's frequent complaint of either one or the other. Each of them spent an hour or so every week washing their 'undies' and putting their hair in rollers, leaving smells of detergent and shampoo. Father and Ken always seemed to leave another kind of smell, which resulted in the tiny window being forced open to its poor maximum. In general, there seemed to be a tacit understanding that men were 'muckier' than women and that the bathroom was really the domain of the females, who allowed the males to make use of it.

Occasionally there might be two of us in the bathroom together: when mother washed my hair before I was able to do it myself (wringing the water out of it fiercely as if it were a tablecloth, hurting my scalp); when I had to be sick and father exercised his St John's Ambulance training by keeping my hair back and holding my forehead with a firm hand while I retched.

After my brutal initiation into the world of personal hygiene at the hands of my schoolmates, I carved out for myself a regular time of my own in this room, for baths - always quick and uncomfortable, done in limestone-hard water, never like they were in the films, luxurious and full of bubbles - and for hair-washing with the aid of a cup over the little basin. I began to take note of my face in the mirror, to wonder if the various bits were as they should be, as prescribed in my sisters' magazines.

One Saturday morning when mother was at the shops, in the bathroom I saw to my horror a reddish-brown fresh stain in my knickers. Having two older sisters I could not but know what this was. I had seen one or another of them, many a time, coming into the living-room with an aggrieved air about her and a small white package hidden in her hand which she thrust into the heart of the coals, after first making sure that no men were around, or if they were that they weren't looking. I had seen Doreen doubled up with a hot-water bottle clutched to her stomach, and heard from mother that she had her 'monthlies, poor girl'. So when my turn came, I was not mystified; nonetheless, I began to cry. I sat there alone and cried, perhaps for half an hour, cried for the end or the beginning of something, I did not know, I only knew that it was a sorrow. When mother came home she found she had to go out again and returned with an elastic belt and a packet of pads. In the bathroom she showed me how to put this awful harness on and her words were full of doom and gloom:

"It's a messy business. See what women have to put up with."

I, too, began to take shameful white packets down to the fire. Occasionally, it would be Saturday afternoon, after closing time, and having run out of packets, mother would press half a crown in my hand and say the dreaded words:

"Go up to Mr Jones's back door and knock. He'll let you have a packet".

The awful embarrassment, having to pronounce the words *sanitary towels*. I didn't like Mr Jones to begin with, he had those glasses with lenses that made his eyes seem enormous and he never smiled at anyone.

"*Go on*, I'm not going out again, your legs are younger than mine."

There was nothing for it but to go along the back lane and knock on the rear door of the chemist's shop. I had the idea that Mr Jones lived in the shop, because he was always there, and even on Saturday afternoon when it was closed he still had his white coat on. He opened the door a fraction, just enough to see with one eye, and his fish gaze moved down from adult face level to my level and I said the words with my face burning, holding out the coin. Saying nothing, just giving a barely perceptible nod, he closed the door on me and I waited. A minute later, his arm reached through the little space he had opened again and handed me the packet, opening his palm for the coin.

"'Nk you." He never answered, just shut the door and bolted it; I could hear the scrape of the iron on the inside.

"Do you remember Mr Jones the chemist?" mother asked me twenty years later. "Well, what do you think, they arrested him, he was taking dirty photos of little kids in his back room. There's no knowing folk, is there? He seemed such a nice polite man, who'd have thought."

In your back room, or in your bathroom, you can engage in your most intimate rituals. Another one to learn was the removal of armpit hair, by means of a smelly, pale blue cream which when it was wiped away brought all the hair with it. The sight of this mess of hair and cream was repulsive to me; what with blood and hair and smells, my whole body began to seem repulsive and problematic. I was given a girdle like the ones my sisters hung up to dry: a tight elastic thing with suspenders hanging from it, to which I learned to attach 'flesh-coloured' stockings (they certainly weren't the colour of *my* white northern flesh) which almost always had ladders in them the next day. Another thing I learned from my sisters was that ladders could be limited in their length by dabbing them with nail polish. I only wore this paraphernalia to school when we did not have games, because I didn't like the idea of undressing with all that on show. Mother bought me chain store bras which always had the wrong kind of cup, and being reduced to tears by the sight of my lumpy breasts under my jumper, in the bathroom I tried stuffing toilet paper into the cup ends to fill them out.

To have a really hot bath, the fire downstairs had to be stoked up for hours, and then you only had as much water as the boiler would hold before it ran cold again. I never had a bath with the water higher than my navel. Daily baths were unheard of; nobody would have ever thought it necessary to apply soap to their skin that often. Sunday was recognised by all as Father's Bath Day: winter or summer, all day long the living room was a furnace of glowing coals that he presided over himself until, before teatime, he went up to the bathroom to prepare this ceremony. Inevitable were mother's comments, every Sunday, out of his hearing:

"He doesn't need it that hot."

"It's not good for you, *that* hot."

And then later, when he had finished, inevitable was her exit, gasping disapproval, from the bathroom with its window and mirrors all steamed up, its towels all damp: "Oh, it's like a blooming sauna in there!"

THE LIVING ROOM

The heart of the house, as the kitchen is in the houses of the rich. The room where all the living was done, all the fun had, all the solemn pronouncements made and all the food eaten, because it also doubled as dining room. There was never a table that did not fold up and have extension 'leaves', because that was the only way to make the dining room disappear when meals were over and other things were to be done. The room was small – oh, how very small! – and had to contain so much.

Do people still have wallpaper? If someone, one of the various owners, stripped the walls in this room before painting, how many layers of paper would he have found? Two at the very least: one with a large trellis and roses pattern and another, on a higher level, with a beige ears-of-corn pattern. Two words come into my mind that have lain dormant there all of my adult foreign life, having found little need for them: skirting-board and picture rail. Hung on the latter, no pictures but a horizontal mirror with a curved edge, tilting slightly forward, where Ken combed and recombed and recombed his Elvis 'quiff', where mother powdered her nose and blushed when father, waiting, tried to give her a kiss ("Mind my hair!")

There were no pictures, until I brought home one of my own in later years, a mediocre still-life *à la* Cézanne which I'd done in coloured chalks, and I was surprised at how proudly they hung it up on the left of the fireplace. Not long after, on one of my visits, there was another framed picture on the right of the fireplace: a reproduction of a painting that I had seen many times on my visits to the city Art Gallery. The scene is in a Royalist house during the English Civil War and the Roundhead soldiers have taken over the house and are questioning the little boy about his Royalist father's whereabouts. The child stands bravely upright in the centre of the picture. He has been brought up to believe that honesty is a virtue, and does not realise the gravity of the situation. The littleness of the boy, his blonde hair and blue suit highlight his innocence. To save his father, he must lie to the men questioning him. The little girl on the left, who appears to understand more than he does, and is crying, is probably his sister.

"Ken brought that for us," said mother, "It's nice, isn't it?"

I peered closely and read the title underneath.

When Did You Last See Your Father?

Beneath this picture, a Singer sewing machine, shiny black with a cast-iron base, where I loved to swing the treadle up and down with my foot. Doreen was the only one who made use of this machine, turning out skirts and dresses with a natural dexterity, even obtaining a dummy to try things out on, her paper patterns spread over the floor. It was taken for granted in those days that if you bought something that was too long or too tight you would know how to make alterations to it, or add a collar, or buy a length of cotton and make something you wanted from scratch. People still knew how to use their hands - wood and fabric and paper and the satisfaction of a personal skill. A few times I was allowed myself to try to sew a straight line with the needle going *chu-chu-chu* as I turned the handle slowly. When this machine, too, disappeared in the ready-made, plastic Sixties, it was replaced with a glass-fronted cabinet of lacquered wood where mother kept the 'best' teacups; relics themselves of a time when *craft* did not mean only a boat.

In the heart of the house, the heart of the room was a large, wooden-framed fireplace with blue-decorated tiles on either side of the 'bonnet', which was made of brass and had a dent in it made by mother with the poker one day in a long-forgotten moment of anger. In the hearth, separated from the hearth-rug by a 'fender', there was the famous poker, a black brush and a brass coal scuttle which was always full and had to be refilled every day, or every evening, from the coal shed in the back garden. Each evening, before going to bed, father 'laid' the fire for the next day, in his meticulous mathematician's fashion. First, pages of old newspaper were twisted into sausages and folded into V shapes; these were laid down in the fireplace, and covered by a layer of thin strips of wood, which came from a mysterious shop called the 'chandler's'; on top of the wood, the smallest bits of coal were piled, one by one. Father laid each thing as if it were a piece of a puzzle and had only one possible correct position. (When, occasionally, mother did it, she stacked things up with the efficient haste of busy women, and the fire burned just the same.) In the morning, the fire was lit, usually by father again, by putting a match to the paper peeking out at the bottom. Sometimes, if it was slow, he would engage in what he called 'getting it to draw', which meant holding a double-page piece of newspaper against the fireplace so that the draught sucked it tight and made the flames leap.

"You'll have the house on fire doing that," said mother, but he was proud of his magic feat. When the paper threatened to show a tinge of pale brown he would whip it away, crumple it up and throw it in the flame.

The fire, once lit, had to be monitored and fed constantly. Letting the fire go out was one of the worst crimes, as no doubt it was in the Stone Age. The fire fed the boiler and the boiler meant hot water, of a limited amount. The only source of heat we had was this fire, and all the upstairs rooms were cold, until in later years father relented and installed one-bar electric fires on the walls of the bedrooms and the bathroom.

Sometimes, in wet weather, mother would bring into the living room a wooden construction – the 'clothes horse' – that unfolded into three wings and was placed around the fire to have damp washing draped upon it. The washing slowly dried and we waited behind it for the heat to be restored to us.

Many a quiet afternoon I spent sitting on the hearthrug, stroking the cat and succumbing to the fascination of the flames as they slowly scoured out raging caverns in the heap of coals that by imperceptible shifts and crumblings gradually diminished in size and power. Coal produces ash, lots of it. Getting rid of the ashes was the worst job and could not be hurried if you wanted to prevent the fine dust from flying around the room. This was often mother's job, and she was there down on her knees when I foolishly chose that moment to talk about Staying On.

I loved school. My tie to knot, the brown satchel to fill, even the hated hat to stuff in a pocket until it was necessary to wear it – I always thought of the day ahead as being something sure and safe. The scarred and elbow-polished desk where I stored my books was like a stone pillar standing at the centre of my 'other' world. The quadrangle I crossed every morning (the very name *quadrangle* was a joy to me) to go to assembly enclosed me with care. At four o'clock, while others hurtled out of the gates, I sometimes went up to the library and sat there for an hour, reading about – oh, everything and anything! This routine went on comfortably for five years and it seemed to me it would always be so. But then suddenly I was sixteen and a letter was put into my hands, into the hands of each one of us in the class, to take home to our parents and to be signed and returned.

I knew that I would have to fight her. Sitting on the bus going home, I looked around me at the people without seeing them, saying in my heart, "She won't stop me, she won't!"

"Well, I don't know, I'm sure…"

"Only I've got to take the form back by the end of the week."

Standing there in my navy blue uniform, I watched mother raking out the grate, shovelling the ashes into a bucket. She didn't get up, didn't turn around to see the form in my hand, just went on shoveling, and each scrape of the metal shovel was a sign of scorn for what I was wanting.

"It's another two years, isn't it, and there's the uniform, things wear out and they don't come cheap you know."

"I won't need anything else." Frayed cuffs and collars and blouses too tight across the chest were a small price to pay.

Scrape, scrape. "The others were earning good money at your age."

"Everyone else is staying on."

I tried to speak calmly, but I was raging against that crouched, impenetrable back. I always seemed to see her from behind: leaning over the sink, bent over the table, hoovering the carpet, making the beds, she was always bending over or walking away from me. On rare days of high summer, when it was possible to wear dresses with short sleeves, the unfamiliar sight of mother's bare arms was a source of strange fascination for me: white, robust, with brown freckles, she kept them folded across her body as she sat in her chair, and I did not know how it would feel to be enfolded by them.

A dream haunted my nights for a while during my early adolescence. I was looking for my mother, all through the house. I knew she was there somewhere, because I could hear her voice; I even caught glimpses of her - a cardigan sleeve, the back of her brown hair - through the half-open doors, but every time I ran into a room where I felt sure to find her, she was gone. Only just; the air in the room would be tingling, somehow full of her presence and yet she was always gone and I knew I would never be able to catch her up. Every room was empty where she should be.

For a week or two, during my last year in primary school, it was not a dream but real; she was not there at all. I came home from school one afternoon, opened the back door and found Ida in the kitchen, waiting for me.

"Hello Jean," she said in a bright, too bright voice, so I knew something was wrong. Before I could ask, she went on, "Mum's not here. She's been taken bad and gone to hospital. Don't you worry, she'll be home soon."

Father, very quiet, reiterated the same thing, but nobody said just how she had been 'taken bad', and I was not taken to see her while she was away. We sat around the table and ate what Ida served up, in almost silence, and after meals everybody, except father, seemed to have a reason to go out of the house, as if they could not bear to stay there where there was such a gaping hole for all sorts of dangers to blow through. I took refuge, as always, in my books, peering over them as father passed back and forth. We all seemed like strangers in a hotel, saying goodnight in a strained manner and avoiding all but fugitive eye contact.

I crossed Ken on the stairs and paused, my book clutched to my chest.

"What's up with mum?" I whispered.

"She's sick," he said, wanting to push past me, not to talk about it.

"What's she got?" I insisted.

"She's just having a rest," he said and went on downstairs.

He had heard that phrase during the doctor's visit. They had taken mother in to *have a little rest*. That was all we knew. I tried not to look at her made-up bed and burrowed into my own in search of safety. Never had we lived such silent days in that house. Then, one afternoon, I came up the path again from school and saw from a distance her head once more bent over the kitchen sink and she greeted me as on every other school day, as if nothing had ever happened. She bore no signs of physical trauma, no bandages, no plasters; the only reference she ever made to her absence was to say how kind everybody had been to her, how understanding.

Now the ashes slid into the bucket, but no matter how slowly and carefully she poured them from the shovel, a faint grey cloud always rose up towards her face. Her look was concentrated, her lips tight.

"Mrs Owen's daughter's got a good job in the bank now, she likes it."

Scrape, scrape. At last, she sat back on her heels and gave a sigh.

"Oh well, you'll have to see what your father says, I suppose."

He said, of course, that I was to stay, despite my having so bitterly disappointed him, right there in the living room three years before that, and all due to what mother quaintly called 'all that book-learning'.

It had been a Sunday morning in the living-room, everyone in their usual routines, nobody suspecting that I was about to upset mine forever. In those years we had a school lesson called "Scripture", with an intelligent woman who encouraged us to discuss and argue about what was contained in the Bible. After one particular lesson I had stayed for some moments to ask her some things - digging and prying away at her belief, wanting so much for her to give me the key, the *proof* that would make it all clear so that I wouldn't have to argue any more, but my questions and her answers ended - as they always do - with her smiling and saying, "You simply have to have Faith," and the smile seemed to me like that of one who belongs to a secret society, shutting you out because you don't know the password, and it just wasn't enough.

"Aren't you ready yet?" said father in surprise, coming in

to the living room with his hat already on and holding his gloves, dressed for going to church.

"I'm not going."

He was shocked into immobility.

"What do you mean, you're not going?"

"I'm not going. That's all."

"Why ever not?"

"I don't want to."

"I don't know what you mean. Come along, get ready, it's late enough as it is," he said brusquely, attaching no weight to what I had said, brushing it aside like a childish whim.

"I'm not going."

On either side of the table we faced each other, equally shocked by my daring. Somehow I knew that much more than going to church was at stake, and I stood my ground. He talked as if I were not in full possession of my senses.

"Don't be silly now, get your coat. I shan't tell you again."

"No, I'm *not going.*"

He hardly knew how to cope with the novelty of it. There was silence for a few moments. Pulling on one of his gloves:

"Now, are you going to be sensible? This is the last time I'm asking you. Are you going to get ready or not?"

Are you going to break my heart or not? Forgive me, but I have to follow my own. Off he went down the path, very straight-backed, very alone, to his pew, until mother rejoined him in their later years to pray for the peace that never came back to them.

That table stood opposite the fireplace, with its hidden wings that came up and down two or three times a day. At Christmas, they stayed up nearly all the time, because after eating there were games to be played, Tiddlywinks, Monopoly, Snakes and Ladders, Snap... But first the dinner, table flat out, all lights blazing, all chairs in place, everybody squeezed in. Normally two chairs stayed out in the hall and when they had to be used in the living room, there was so little space left that once you sat in your chair you had to stay there, or else disturb the whole show to get out. When I was small enough to need two cushions to bring my mouth above the level of the table, the food was brought in and out by what were, to me, three tall women - mother, Ida and Doreen. Things were spooned onto my plate and father sat on my right side at the head of the table, sharpening the carving knife with a long metal rod, *Shiik, shiik, shiik....*

When it was to his liking, he made a pretence of going for my throat with it, which sent me squealing backwards in my chair.

"For what we are about to receive..."

But at Christmas there was the Pudding; and in the Pudding was a 'thripny bit', a small yellow coin with eight sides, worth three pennies. When I joyfully found it on my spoon and licked off the puddingy bits, did I really not know that they had contrived for me to have it? There were crackers to be pulled and daft things to be read out, and coloured paper hats to be worn. How strange to see father in a funny paper hat! Later, in my adolescent snobbery, I refused to put one of these on my head and sat without, spoiling the party and longing, in my secret heart, to be part of it. Christmas decorations were limited to this room: father put them up with a ruler for mathematical precision, corner to corner, corner to central light, over the mirror and around the door frame, and for a few years, before the tatty plastic Sixties came in, we had a real tree that lost its needles and I was lifted up to put the star on the top of it, just like in the best of films. With the tree and all the paper of the decorations and the parcels, and the leg-to-leg furniture in front of the open hearth, it was a wonder if nothing caught fire.

After some years, when they had all gone to their respective homes except me, Christmas became a lukewarm affair little different from any other day - gone the tree, the decorations, the laughter and even the turkey. Mother bought a tiny plastic tree complete with shabby little bells, which could be folded up and put away until the following year, and stood it on the mantelpiece. Instead of the board games there was only the TV, with its children in hospital on Christmas morning, the Queen at three o'clock and various bouts of singing and dancing after tea. Sometimes Doreen or Ida would return home, with stiff, awkward husbands in tow, on Boxing Day. We exchanged our presents in little packages, mumbling the ritual words and pretending, for a few seconds, to be happily surprised.

Everything was winding down. The only thing that did

not change, that marked the end of one year and the start of another, was the sound of the ships. We lived near the river, and on New Year's Eve, at midnight precisely, all the boats that were in port sounded their sirens. The front door would be opened, despite the cold, to let the sound – and the New Year – come in, and standing there in the hallway, sometimes with fog rolling across the open doorway in the light of the streetlamp, listening to the booming and hooting, I was always oddly full of quiet joy. The siren of ships means departure, the immense ocean spreading out before your mind – a new world!

Before the television arrived, games of all kinds meant that people engaged with one another, laughed together, used their brains. Sometimes everyone joined in, like at Christmas, when even mother was persuaded to sit down in her apron ("but I don't want anything with a lot of thinking in it"), and sometimes there were only two players, and occasionally even just one, playing patience. On wet Sunday afternoons, father and Ken sat by the fireside over a fold-up card table and a pack of pink-backed cards.

"Can I play?" I wormed my childish way in.

"Not now," said Ken, brushing me away, jealously protecting this precious man-to-man moment. They sat hunched over, holding their cards close, glancing at each other's faces suspiciously, smiling ironically. I looked down at the long board and the matchsticks marching up and down it in little holes. They spoke a strange secret language:

"Fifteen two, fifteen four and six and two's eight."

"I can learn it too," I pestered.

"No!" Ken turned on me, "GO AWAY!"

"Daaad…"

But to my surprise there was no help from there either. No doubt about it: they did not want me.

"Fifteen two, fifteen four…"

I was impressed by the seriousness. They slapped their winning cards down like knives going into the table and they didn't look round or get up to eat or drink or talk about other things in the middle as they did when we all played together. For half an hour they were locked in combat. When Ken won he was radiant, but father called it beginner's luck. When he won he lit his pipe and puffed at the ceiling.

"Better luck next time, lad."

"I wish you wouldn't smoke that thing in here," said mother, coming in between them to rake the coals in the fireplace.

The shabby Sixties brought a new piece of furniture into the living room, an obligatory purchase, to stand the television on. When it was delivered and placed in the corner beside the fireplace, its poor quality and design stood out against the massive, Victorian woodwork of the mantelpiece. It had four tapering legs and two front sliding doors which stuck when they were in movement. A few blows of a man's fist would have reduced the thing to firewood.

"It's a bargain," said mother, "everyone's got them now."

And so this flimsy altar became the focal point of the room, with its aggressive tin god atop, and the room's seating was slightly shifted so that we no longer looked at each other, but at the television. Ah, the seating – if the others hadn't gone out with friends in the evenings, if everybody had been in the house and in the living room at the same time, where on earth would we all have sat? Personal interests ensured that this never occurred, and on the rare occasions when Doreen or Ida stayed in, they were always busy upstairs washing and rollering their hair or washing their stockings and hanging them in the boiler cupboard to dry. What were we looking at? The first brown-framed heavy television set was brought into the living-room when I was nine years old. (What did we do in the evenings before that? We listened to the radio, we played cards and Monopoly, we talked to one another. Mother was the first to describe how the television was changing our life: "Good grief, you can't even open your mouth any more with this damn thing"). Of course, it was not ours, it was rented, a few shillings a week.

The first thing I saw, while the technician who delivered it was still putting his final touches, was a horse race; it seemed the most fascinating thing in the world at that moment, keeping me glued in my seat for half an hour. Two years later I watched, with a certain juvenile perplexity, the grey smudgy image of a number of men in a far-off place constructing a high wall which apparently merited a long commentary and conveyed to me a vague sense of dreadful importance, the memory of which came back to me three decades later as I sat in a different living-room and watched the demolition of the same wall, now understanding perfectly its fundamental role in all our lives.

We soon all found our favourite programmes and time began to be regulated by these; my brother rushed home from work to see *Yogi Bear* ("all the blokes do – never miss it") and I fell in love with Little Joe of *Bonanza*; mother loved the Hollywood films that were shown after lunch at weekends. My sisters were old enough to have escaped the insidious grip of the idol in the corner, continuing to prefer evenings at friends' houses or at the dance hall.

And father? He came home on his moped so late from work in the evenings, arriving after we had all eaten, often cold and wet, that I don't think he cared two hoots what passed before his eyes in the few hours left to him before he had to go to bed early in order to get on that moped again the next dark morning. Only on Saturday afternoons, sometimes with Ken, would he take an active interest in wrestling, snooker and sometimes football. It was one of the few ways of communication between them: not looking at each other, but looking at something together, which might be said of most families from the Sixties onwards.

A new word began to fly around: satire. Taking the piss out of big shots, as my brother defined it. Humour began to be less pie-in-the-face and more think-about-it, and herein lay the wedge between generations. Our parents 'didn't GET

IT', they were too slow, they were SQUARE, they began to be left behind. We got smart, cocky, full of scorn for their old style humour and tastes: *The Black and White Minstrel Show*, it was unthinkable that your friends should find out it was seen in your house!

But we *all* sat down together, at half-past seven on Mondays and Wednesdays, the table cleared and the dishes washed, to watch *Coronation Street*. Not even mother wanted to say anything for half an hour. That was US, there on telly! People like us were suddenly visible, audible, we counted, we mattered. They spoke like us and worried about the same things, and between episodes their doings and misdeeds were discussed among us as if they were friends just a few streets away and only in need of our wise advice. This feeling was intensified, at least in my own mind, by the fact that a small street of local shops, just around the corner, was called Coronation Drive.

At the same time, four successful hairy boys from across the river were putting us all on the map, making a mint of money and giving us a sense of pride in our origins. All of a sudden, it was fun and fashionable to have on your TV programme someone who spoke *like that*, someone who spoke like us. We could cock a snook at the folks in London for once.

One afternoon, after school had finished, my best friend Jenny and I, still in our uniforms, took a bus and a ferry and squeezed ourselves into a crowded square where robust housewives in raincoats and headscarves looked daggers at us – "Ay, you, stop pushin', I've bin 'ere since ten o'clock this mornin!" All faces were turned up to a small balcony on the Victorian façade of the Town Hall, where four black-suited figures jostled out and stared at us, seeming almost intimidated, fresh from their triumphant American visit. Cheering, waving, screaming, the crowd let loose its enthusiasm: if they'd been down among us I think they would have been torn to pieces. George was Jenny's and Paul was mine. *Is he looking at me? He is! He's looking right over here!*

There was more to it than a few good songs. It was a signal, for those who were waiting for one, that the repetition of a way of life was not inevitable, that you could break the pattern, you could dare, even if you started out with nothing but your dreams and a few ounces of talent. I picked up that signal, cast off from the dock and began to veer away off course, drifting out into the open sea, starting on my 'journey to Ithaca'. I did not know what it might mean to Ken, that signal, if he picked it up too. Whatever hopes it might have started singing in him were extinguished right away by a wrong early marriage and divorce.

That marriage was announced in this room, joyless and doomed from the start. Still at school, absorbed in my own doings, heedless of the drama collecting about me, the first I knew of it was when there was a Sunday afternoon visit by a girl I had never seen before and mother got the best teacups out of the cupboard and washed them. The living room had never seemed so small and stuffy. As usual, sensing the tension in the air, I made myself part of an armchair and watched from behind a book, as through the half-closed curtains the afternoon sun reached in to the fireplace and quenched the weak superfluous flames. I pretended to be reading, feeling I should not be there yet too curious to go elsewhere, full of wonder and fear at this event, this odd thing that was making the air disagreeable and heavy to breathe. Father sat on a dining chair with his arms folded, looking at the fire. His tie was knotted firmly and he cleared his throat noisily. Ken, with his elbows on his knees, flicked ash into the fire and he, too, stared at the flames. He was wearing his best suit. The girl in the red dress and white patent leather shoes, perched uncomfortably next to him on the edge of the sofa, stared at the carpet. He hardly knew her.

To me, they looked like two people sitting on a bus.

Mother had waylaid me on the stairs before the girl arrived, to make sure I understood and wouldn't say anything out of line. She was irritable and frowning; she seemed almost angry with *me*, at having to speak to me at all.

"They'll have to get married. She's going to have a baby."

I stared.

"I'm just telling you. So you know. Don't ever let boys mess about with you."

"No," I said, but it seemed like news of an earthquake on the other side of the world. Who and where these boys were, that might want to 'mess about', I did not know: I went every day to a school full of girls; I stayed in every evening. At weekends I went my solitary way, discovering the art gallery, the museum, department stores, and sometimes I took a sketchbook with me to quiet places where I could draw, never dreaming of the risk I was running. I went into the park and drew the roots of trees bursting through stone; I went down to the riverside, clambered down the rocks and sat there for an hour, totally alone, watching birds and boats until the light began to fade. Walking back through the wood towards the road, I met a police car prowling around; they stared at me -

"What're you doing here, love?"

"Just walking." I showed my sketchbook, embarrassed.

"You don't want to come down here, love, there's funny blokes about, you get off home, now."

So it was that I began to learn the *law* - that unwritten, yet cast-iron law that endows 'funny blokes' with more freedom of movement than 'serious' women.

Mother was the only one in motion, back and forth between the kitchen and the living room, making tea, setting cups, smoothing the cloth, smoothing, smoothing, not saying in words but in her compressed lips:

Common little piece.

She hid her face in the kitchen (the world is falling about your ears? Make the tea, clean the floor, wash the windows) and with her whole self shouting one big NO she listened to the inevitable phrases of false hope that father murmured at intervals.

Make a go of it.
Stick at your job.
A few sacrifices.

When mother swung the door open with her foot and planted the tray noisily on the table, the girl looked up with a tentative smile, trying to make the link, woman-to-woman. She was wearing bright red lipstick that contrasted strongly with her beehive black hair. Mother smiled with her mouth.

She's not his type. Tarted up like that.

She shoved the biscuits around on their plate in a superfluous dance and stirred up the peaceful sugar in its bowl.

"I'll be able to go on working for a bit before the baby comes."

The girl's unfamiliar, strongly-accented voice fell strangely in the room, like snow in a shaken glass paperweight, changing the landscape. She was very young, not even twenty yet, daughter of poor Irish immigrants, those who landed at the port and stayed there forever, due to lack of means or of imagination. A new dress and shoes, a night out, a few beers and a lad with an Elvis hairdo and nice eyes, to try and make a life out of.

But he hardly knew her.

On the day they married, she wore a yellow dress and those white shoes. Four-thirty in the afternoon - outside, shoppers and vans and buses filling up with schoolchildren, litter piling up in the bins and gutters, people thinking what to have for dinner, what to watch on telly; inside, beneath the cold, unforgiving gothic columns of the strange church we all huddled in silence: Ken, all in black, me straight from school in my uniform, mother and father and another woman in a brown coat, tearful and timid and alone, who was the girl's mother. In silence we heard the bride pitter-patter up the aisle, her steps echoing loudly (there was no music) and when she arrived at Ken's side, in her lemon-coloured dress she looked like a butterfly on a piece of coal. Nobody looked at anybody, the priest mumbled in his book; he had seen it all before. Mother conversed with herself, her face contorted. I was watching my brother. How very pale he was in his black suit, and very still. Suddenly it stopped being a distant event and came flying up close to me. I knew that he didn't want this. I understood, and glancing quickly at my parents I understood that nobody wanted this, nobody at all, not even the girl in the yellow dress. My heart began to thump. The priest had said something and the girl had answered, and now he was saying it to Ken, and there, just there in the tiny pause, I saw that the girl lifted her elbow and nudged his arm.

THE KITCHEN

How many things can be got into a tiny kitchen! This, more than anything, was the room that marked the passing of the years.

To begin with, wall-to-wall linoleum and a mat in front of the door. One step down into the back garden, one small window above the sink, which was a thick white rectangular one with a wooden draining board. The pans were lined up on two open shelves above the cooker and to one side of the cooker was a wicker container on legs, which held potatoes and other vegetables. Next to this, in a corner, was a door that opened onto the space with a deeply sloping ceiling formed by the stairs above it. Here were stored deckchairs for rare sunny days, the mower, buckets and brushes. For some reason this place - which I trembled to enter, thinking it full of spiders - was called the Glory Hole ("It'll be in the gloriole if you look.") Opposite the sink - just two steps would do it

– there stood a small wooden cupboard with a drawer and two cupboards below and shelves above which were closed by a door with a mesh front. Here on the shelves, milk and margarine and cheese were kept. There was no fridge, nor was there a washing machine. Mother washed by hand for six people and sent the sheets to the laundry.

Opposite the cooker was what existed before the spin dryer: the mangle. You may see one of these in any museum devoted to Victorian life: a massive cast iron stand, chest high, and two thick wooden rollers with a fraction of space between them; at the side, a handle which, when turned, set the rollers in motion in opposite directions, crushing whatever – a sheet, a towel, a shirt – was placed between them. The water that was squeezed out of them fell noisily into a bucket placed underneath. Even the buckets were metal; there was little, yet, that was made of plastic, and women had to be strong-armed.

Once a week mother struggled with heavy wet washing that had to be heaved, dripping, from the sink by means of wooden tongs to a bucket and from the bucket, one by one, fed into the maw of the mangle. She was a small woman and there were six of us. One day, hurrying, she fed her finger to the mangle and when I saw her sitting at the table with a mustard poultice making her cry, I cried too.

She frowned at me. "Oh, shut up, you! What are you whining for, it's not *your* finger!"

But I was small enough for it to *feel* like my finger.

For a few years she still baked cakes and apple pies; there was a big cream-coloured ceramic bowl that was filled with mixture once a week and I was allowed to run my finger around the inside before it was washed. Then, once again, it was the Shoddy Sixties that moved into the kitchen and changed the landscape there, too. Mother came home one day full of wonder and enthusiasm: a new store had appeared in the town centre - a *supermarket* where you could go with a five-pound note and still come out with change! This magical place went by the appealing name of Kwiksave and came to be fondly called Kwikky's by mother - "I'll just pop down to Kwikky's".

She took me with her one day and we trudged up and down the aisles made by bare wooden shelves that were full of the cardboard boxes the goods had travelled in and remained in - there was no flashy advertising, and prices were handwritten on makeshift cards. None too clean underfoot, it was little more than a warehouse, this forerunner of empires to come. Most of the food was tinned and our kitchen began to fill up: tinned peaches, tinned carrots, tinned beans, even tinned potatoes. The pudding bowl was put away and never came out again. A new kind of dessert was offered to us - you simply opened a packet of whitish powder, mixed it up with milk and *abracadabra* you had a 'Lemon Delight' or a 'Raspberry Joy'.

All this sounded the death knell for Bill and his Van.

Bill was a middle-aged man in a green cotton coat who,

once a week, drove his van around the streets selling his own produce to housewives like mother. His was a kind of aproned harem; he was an attractive man and there was much banter and get-away-with-you exchanges, all, of course, directed at sales. His arrival was one of mother's highlights of the week, even though she often cursed him.

"He's sold me two bad 'uns, look!"

"If you don't keep an eye on him, he'll diddle you!"

But when he invited her to climb up inside and have a look, she blushed and declined; heaven knows what he might get up to behind the caulis.

Bill and his Van vanished from the landscape soon after the apple pies.

But what mostly came out of the kitchen, as in all houses all over the land, was tea: strong, orange-coloured tea, for breakfast, during lunch, after lunch, during 'tea-time' (which meant dinner, not the five-o'clock ritual so beloved of tourists and the British upper classes in films), for supper, and at any other time when circumstances seemed to demand it - a visitor, a crisis to be faced: *I'll make us some tea.* A friend of mine, in later years, said they must put something in the tea to explain the apathy or passivity of the British in situations which would have other nations in bloody riots or civil wars. I have lived away from my country for most of my adult life among cafés and cappuccinos, but I have never failed to begin my day with a mug of hot tea with milk, which seems as essential to me as getting dressed. On my home visits, which were increasingly spaced out, tea was the first thing to be offered, even before my coat was off. But there came a time, just after Ken's divorce, when I was the one to go into the kitchen and organise the tea, because mother was sitting on the couch like a zombie. After hours of delayed travel in the coldest month of the year, by plane, train and bus, I had arrived at last with my case, to be greeted by her at the door with indifference.

"Oh, it's you. 'lo."

As if I were living in the next street and came every day. She left me in the hall and walked back into the living-room, sat down where she had been before and picked up her knitting. I left my case by the door, took off my coat and sat in the armchair.

"How's father?"

"Eh?" It was as if my words reached her with difficulty through something dense. "Oh, *he's* all right. He's gone to the doctor's, he'll be back soon."

Knit, knit. She roused herself enough to ask, "Had a good journey, then?"

My account of my day frayed into nothing when I realised she was not following me. I got up. I would have to be mother, if she could not.

"I'll make us some tea, shall I?"

"Yes, go on, you can do."

It was while I was getting things together in the kitchen that I found the card. Looking for biscuits I opened the cabinet and searched for the blue square tin, down below in the cupboards among things that were in reserve, like bags of sugar, flour, salt and of course tea. Lifting out the tin I saw there was a paper behind a box of sugar lumps. I pulled it out; it was a large white envelope, unsealed, and inside it was a birthday card, one of those with a large, padded red heart on the front surrounded by drawings of ribbons and little flowers; *To My Darling* in gold lettering above the heart. It was one of those that some people might give to their boyfriends or girlfriends, or a spouse when the honeymoon was not altogether forgotten.

My mind flicked rapidly through the facts: it was nowhere near father's birthday; my mother was not an unattractive woman even in her sixties, but that she should have a lover, to the point of acquiring such a card, was as likely as me becoming Miss World; there were two birthdays in the coldest month - my brother's and mine; mine was yet to come, but I knew it wasn't for me. Ken's had just gone. Yet she hadn't had the courage to send it to her son, she must have had last-minute doubts herself about her choice. I put it back and carried in the tea-tray with the biscuits.

That night, in my old bed unable to sleep, listening to my parents snoring behind the wall, I remembered a strange journey I had been forced into making with mother. When I was about ten, father had a minor operation which kept him in hospital for five days. On one of those nights I was woken from my sleep by mother bending over the bed and shaking me.

"Get dressed, you'll have to come with me."

It seemed like the middle of the night to me, but in fact I had only been sleeping for an hour or so. My school clothes were the nearest things, so I pulled them on and we left the house, just mother and I, in the darkness. It was summer, Doreen and Ida were both on holiday together with their boyfriends, so nobody knew how we walked in the night streets to the bus stop and took a late bus down to the station. Mother gave me no explanation and I was too sleepy and rushed to talk, but the night air soon shook me wide awake and I asked,

"Where are we going?"

Mother did not look at me, walking determinedly through the lamplit streets.

"To find Ken."

I said nothing more the whole way. The city streets scared and fascinated me; I had never seen them like that before. While the sickly yellow lights shone down eerily upon emptiness I had always been sleeping, I'd had no idea of the existence of this illuminated stage all set up and ready - for what, for whom?

In the underground station our footsteps echoed loudly on the platform; there were few people about, it was too early yet for the night owls to be going home, they were all still in the clubs and restaurants or drinking their last rounds in the crowded pubs. A man stood at the far end of the platform muttering to himself and on the other side of the tracks three boys sat laughing and smoking. The man lumbered slowly along towards us and I grasped a fold of mother's coat as I had not done since I was five, but mother seemed almost oblivious to her surroundings. If an entire army had come marching along the platform pointing bayonets, I don't think she would have taken much notice. There was no fear in her just then.

In a few moments we were in the city centre and there was still a great deal of life going on. People were walking and laughing, some of them clearly drunk, all with a mask-like quality to their faces under the streetlights. The sound of the traffic was comforting, reminding me of the normal day-life. A group of men suddenly came shoving and jeering around a corner so that mother had to step off the pavement to get by, and I felt the bulk of them leaning at us, the wave of stale beer, the small silence while they sized us up before resuming their banter.

Mother seemed to know exactly where she was going. She must have scouted out the place during the day on one of her shopping trips. She gripped my wrist and we turned into a narrow side street where the lights and traffic were suddenly extinguished and it was dark and rubbishy underfoot. A single doorway at the far end was lit by an overhead lamp. A white-faced man stood there and a few other people were talking and laughing around the doorway. From somewhere deep beneath us came a regular muffled sound, a heavy beating of music. My heart began to thump too. I pulled back but mother went on just the same in the darkness, keeping hold of my arm. The white-faced man stared at us.

He'll hit her, I thought, he'll kill us both.

Then - terrible! - mother let go of my arm and walked up to the man.

She can't go in! She can't leave me here!

"Have you seen my son?"

The man shrugged. She stood there for a moment, uncertain for the first time.

"His name's Ken."

"Dunno, missis."

"I know he's in there!" Her voice rose, and I began to tremble, perhaps with cold.

The man shifted slightly. "Go in an 'ave a look if yer want."

Don't! Don't!

Everything seemed to be in the balance for a moment and then mother seemed to sag, as if she had come to the end of her courage and energy. She looked around, fully conscious, and saw me standing there.

"Come on."

"Where are we going now?"

"We're going home."

I fell asleep immediately on getting into bed, and in the morning it all seemed like a dream.

The mesh-fronted wooden cabinet was replaced by a larger blue and white one with a front that dropped down on two arms and became a formica-topped work surface. It seemed the height of modernity and kept mother happy for months, and I got used to pulling down the top and making myself a cheese sandwich on it as soon as I came home from school. The old wooden cabinet had had a drawer which was full of all kinds of small, possibly useful things, and the new cabinet had two drawers, so all this stuff was transferred to one of them and the other one gradually began to fill up with similar stuff: light bulbs, elastic bands, sticky tape, wall hooks, carpet tacks, tubes of glue, electric plugs, lengths of string, batteries, bottle tops, small boxes things had been bought in… I have lived in many houses and I have always had one of these drawers, which seems to create itself without my realising it.

There was, in the Sixties, still no washing-machine, but a compromise: a boiler - about the size of a washing-machine, it was nothing but a metal box that could be filled with detergent and water by a hose from the tap, plugged in and heated up, as if it were a great kettle. A cross-arm inside then waggled the washing about. But mother's arm was still needed to get the stuff out, always by means of the long wooden tongs to avoid scalding herself. Six of us and never a washing-machine, never a fridge. Father's total command of finances was combined with Victorian thrift values. If you wanted a thing you paid for it and took it home, or you did without it.

Getting stuff on the *never-never* was definitely out, so, from the house itself downwards, we did without. If mother resented heaving steaming clothes from boiler to sink, or filling a bucket with cold water to put the milk in during hot summer days, she never said it. Only at the very end, alone and somewhat bewildered in the bank for the first time, she gave me her opinion.

"You know, when we got married, he said to me: "Now don't you worry your head about money – I'll look after all that, you just take care of the children and the house." It wasn't right, that."

I don't know if music is really the food of love, but I think that often food is the measure of love. Beginning at the beginning: I was bottle fed, because according to mother, she had 'none left' for me by that time. She, and she alone, was the maker of food for us all and what she gave, and how much, said volumes about our standing. On Sundays, as it was at Christmas, we were all around the table together and there was the to and fro between the kitchen and the living room. Father cut and served the roast while mother, helped by my sisters, portioned out the vegetables, the lion's share going to my brother. Some things were taken for granted: males eat more than females; males work more than females; they are bigger than us; they need more than us. And yet, as if frightened by her own tendency to feed too much, love too much, she took to hiding loaves "otherwise your brother'll eat the lot in one day". All this measuring out of love, as if there was only a limited amount to go around among so many people: you won't want any more than that, will you; that'll do you for seconds, won't it.

Once I saw her serve up father's supper when he came home very late from work. It was the time when only I was left at home, when my brother's story was driving a rift between our parents, and she was using the weapons available to her. It was a cold November night, with a wind that must have felt like sandpaper to the face of anyone journeying on two wheels for half an hour. She placed on the table a plate holding a tiny rectangular portion of cod with a knob of butter melting on it, saying, at the same time,

"You won't want any bread with that, will you."

It was not a question. Cold, tired and hungry, he looked at the plate and I saw how the hurt held him still in his chair.

"I wouldn't mind a slice or two, if it's not too much trouble."

When, years later, she had him at her mercy as he lay in bed with his mind disintegrating, she would only take upstairs a plate of two sandwiches a day. No wonder he wolfed down everything they set before him in the institution, and even took to stealing from others' plates.

THE FRONT ROOM

In Mrs Gaskell's day it would have been called the Parlour. In theory, it was the 'best' room in the house; in reality, it was the coldest, because it was hardly ever lived in and because a fire was lit in the fireplace only a few times in the year. This room was the same size and had a similar fireplace to the living-room, a great wooden frame embellished with decorative tiles. The window, which looked out onto the front garden and like the one above it upstairs was divided into four panes with smaller ones at the top, had coloured glass inserts similar to those of the small window in the hall. Lace curtains backed up by heavier brown ones ensured that we could not be seen from the street, while we could peer through the lace pattern at others. But rarely did we spend any time in there; most of the time we all lived crushed up in the living-room rather than light another costly fire and consume the 'parlour'.

It came alive at Christmas when we were all still living at home. The big real Christmas tree was placed in there and the paper decorations continued their festoons from the living-room. Gift paper strewn around, carols playing on the radio, for a few hours there was life and laughter in the front room, and I played on the carpet with my small pleasures, the only one left who still did not know the truth about Father Christmas.

The thing in the front room that most captured my attention as a small child was the piano: shiny pedals and yellowed keys with the black ones in twos and threes (I wondered why that was); a flimsy wooden bit to put the music pages on and, in front of the piano, a stool with a green velvety top that opened to show thin, yellowy-brown booklets of music. The player, the only player, was father, who, after trying to interest his first and second children without success, gave up disheartened and did not even try to interest my brother or me. How often, alone in the front room, I plonked away by myself, wanting to unlock the mystery of those keys, and how often have I wished, ever after in my life, that I could sit down and play something to comfort myself in difficult times; my bad luck to be born last!

One day there was a strange man in the front room, sitting at the piano. I slipped in, my infant curiosity fighting my shyness, ("Don't you go bothering him," said mother) and watched him. He was a tall, gangly man with straw-coloured hair that curtained his forehead as he leaned down close to the keyboard, but sideways on with his legs crossed. Despite this odd position, I thought he was going to play something, but all he did was to press the same key over and over again, ten times or more, then another key, over and over, in great monotony, so that I soon tired of the spectacle and left the room.

The piano tuner very soon ceased to visit, and the sound of father playing became no more than a memory as he strove to pilot his way through family life. An efficient, scientific player, concerned with getting the notes right, if he saw the passion in some pieces he held it under control, safe and manageable. Later in his life, when they were a couple alone as they had been in the beginning and went to church again together, he played the organ in the church, and later still, somebody sat where he had sat and played it for him as he lay in his box in eternal silence.

Apart from the piano, there was a fake leather couch, an orangey-brown colour, which also had a pedal like the piano, but when you stepped on it the arm of the couch fell down so you could lie on it. Behind the couch was something called 'the bureau', with a sloping lid that became a desk when you tugged it down, and three drawers underneath that were used by father for storing documents and other mysterious papers and folders, along with a veritable stationery shop. As a small child I was forever pressing the pedal of the couch and opening and closing the desk; they seemed to me to be wonderful things.

There was one single picture in this room, on the wall

above the fireplace, which increased in fascination for me when I grew to an age in which I understood that it represented what we saw ourselves every time we took the ferry across the river to the city centre. It was not an original painting, only a reproduction, but I examined with wonder the brushmarks used to whip up the murky water around the ferry boat, and to fill the sky with menacing cloud. Half of the painting was, indeed, sky, and beyond the boat on the other side of the river, the tall buildings waited, lit up by a shaft of sunlight, promising the up-beat attractions of city streets. It seemed to me, as a child, a wonderful thing to have a painting of a place that you could point to and say 'I've been there, I know what it's like on that boat'. When I stood on the couch to get a closer look, if I stayed there long enough I could almost fancy I was there in the picture, running about on the top deck in the wind...

My favourite sound in all the world has always been the sound of seagulls. Whenever they cry overhead, even if I am walking along a busy shopping street or sitting under a tree in a park, my spirit leaps towards the water and I am, for a brief moment, back on the top deck in the wind. Once every two or three months, we would take the ferry across the river, usually for a special purchase, or, at Christmas, to join in the general festive bustle and even, once, to see a *pantomime*. The journey was part of the pleasure - perhaps, for me as the youngest, not the least part. It began with taking the bus as far as it would go without driving into the water, then buying tickets at a little window in a low, sturdy green and yellow building and passing through a creaking turnstile. Beyond that there was a tunnel, a long straight tube with a vaulted glass roof, along which we had to walk, and the oddest thing about this tunnel, to me, was that it was never the same. Sometimes we walked along it normally, as along a road; the next time we had to stagger upwards as if we were climbing a hill; another time we might have to walk leaning backwards to prevent ourselves tumbling downwards. Thus I learned about tides, and how extreme they can be in some places.

Having got to the end of the tunnel, we found ourselves in a large room which was nothing but a wooden platform with glass and wooden walls and a roof, floating on the water: the *landing stage*. This name puzzled me at first, because I knew that stages were in theatres and meant singing and dancing of some kind, as in the *panto,* but although I looked around continually, nothing struck up and nobody leapt in, among the wet raincoats and bags. We gathered together like cattle in a pen, the mooing and shuffling increasing with every new arrival from the tunnel. People kept craning their necks to see where the ferry was in its crossing, and all the while, like a *basso continuo,* there was a rhythmical creaking of wood and splashing of water. On the boat's arrival, we had to wait while the passengers disembarked into an area separate from us and began their toil up or down the tunnel, then there was a great roll of drums in the heavy iron barrier being pushed aside and we streamed onto the boat.

On certain very windy days, which made mother say, pale-faced, 'I hope it comes soon, I don't like this up and down business", the waves were so high that the gap for getting on and off in the side of the boat became level with the landing stage for only a second or two in its motion. In this perilous condition, the sailors would help the passengers to embark one by one, by holding their arms and counting "One… two… *three!*" and hoisting them aboard at the right second, children and grandmothers included.

In reality, the crossing took no more than ten minutes, but it seemed like a great adventure to me. No way was I going to sit inside, whatever the weather; the only place to be was upstairs, where smooth wooden seats sat back to back, where I could run around the deck and watch the gulls following, sometimes throwing the bits of stale bread that I had brought in a paper bag for that purpose and watching them quarrel over it. The wind threatened to pull my hair out by the roots and my nose and cheeks were rubbed raw, but I wanted it to last, the wind and the gulls crying and swooping, and I was always sorry when the boat heaved itself round for landing, too soon, too soon.

One of my brother's first jobs was working on the construction of one of these boats, laying the decks. It gave me a proud thrill to suppose that the boat we were on at any particular moment might have been *that* one, that I might be walking on the boards that he had helped to lay with his own hands.

The other way to get to the city centre was to take the underground, which only went under the ground for part of its journey and the interest of which, to my mind, was limited to the reading of advertisements in the carriages and of posters on the platforms of the stations. This was the practical transport convenient for city centre shops and offices; the ferry was for those who worked in offices near the riverside, or for romantics. Nobody ever painted a picture of the underground train.

Only my earliest years saw the front room included in my daily life; after that it became the home of my grandmother. There was a stillness here that was hardly ever broken, because there was no continuity of life in it, only occasional bursts of light and sound. Then, for a few years, after we had all left to our various destinies, my grandmother moved into it with her salvaged bits and pieces, for the few years that were left to her, and that is how I best remember it, as Nanna's room.

Nanna was mother's mother and she had been a widow for many years before she came to us. She was the only grandparent I ever knew and was my mental model of grandmothers: a small woman with her white hair in a net, wearing outdated dresses with a brooch at her throat, thick brown stockings and heavy black shoes. She had only one child, and whatever she passed down to her daughter, it was not her face. Only when I saw photographs of my missing grandfather could I see where my mother came from. Nanna's face came to me. A widow of almost eighty, she had nowhere to go when her brother decided to sell the house they were living in and father was the first to insist that we take her in, crowded as we were, and give her the front room to herself.

It was not the first time I had been with mother to the big, echoing station in the city centre to welcome Nanna, she had been to visit two or three times already, but this time it was different, it was special. In the clouds of steam that rolled about our legs she greeted mother enthusiastically and gave me two big kisses, exclaiming about the journey, the weather, the pleasure of being here. I realise now that she must have felt so grateful for her rescue and so anxious to please, in case they should change their minds, that she felt the need to underline her happiness continually.

It is sometimes observed that relations between grandparents and grandchildren are often better than those between parents and children, perhaps because they have a lot in common - they get tired quickly, they have to keep stopping for little snacks, and go to the toilet frequently. They also have a ready sense of humour that goes underground in the middle years of responsibility. This was certainly not the case for me. I was entering my teens and exploded like a volcano with anybody who said the slightest thing against whatever I liked, be it music or dress or food. And there was plenty to criticise, so it seemed. Nanna sat with us in the evening, enclosed in her winged armchair, and pursed her mouth up as the TV paraded before her all that was wrong with modern life, all that jarred against her carefully-tended memories.

"Just look at their hair!"

"That's not real music."

"Scarecrows, some of these girls."

"Dressing up like fellers nowadays."

Getting off the bus one day, coming home from school, I saw Nanna walking ahead of me, about fifty yards away. I did not run to catch her up but lagged behind and watched her with a curious cold detachment. She always wore purple or dark blue and her thin ankles in their dark stockings seemed too slender for the big solid black shoes that she never exchanged for a pair of slippers at home. Her white hair peeped out from beneath a hat belonging to the Forties and her little lace gloves, which were for show rather than any warmth, were the same colour. Nanna refused to use a walking-stick, preferring people to suppose that she was a prudent lady carrying a long umbrella just in case.

I lingered, swinging my school satchel on my shoulder, so that I would not catch up with her and have to talk to her. I did not love the little figure as I watched it wending its tired way along the back lane towards the house. As I watch it all again now, I think how lonely she must have been in her last years, uprooted from her home, neighbours, habits and familiar landmarks and put down in another place where the only point of reference she had was her daughter. No, I did not, because I could not, seize the privilege of having my grandmother near me then, but I saw, I heard, that there was a special something between Nanna and Ken. Not that they spent any time together, not that they ever sat and talked, no, but just in the way he would say, "All right, Nanna?" as he passed through the hall when she was in her doorway, and she would smile and answer, "Hello, Ken my lad." You could tell that they were, somehow, of the same stuff, of the same heart.

Once or twice, when she was out and about, I crept into the front room and looked around, trying to find out about my grandmother surreptitiously, as it were. There was a smell that I could not give a name to, not perfume, not unpleasant either - probably the smell of an old woman's clothes, I think now. A small round table covered with a lacy white cloth; a radio; a high-backed, wooden-armed chair - the three things very close together, her small world in the evenings when she did not want to join us for television. But the thing that I noticed at once was the sand-bell: a little glass container in the shape of a bell filled with strata of different-coloured sands. My enthusiasm for this object was met with indifference by everyone, but it persisted over the years and eventually, somehow, long after she had died, it came into my hands. During my many moves from one home to another, I don't know how, it disappeared, but I can clearly remember the surprising weight of it in my hand and the delicate shades of the sand.

She was not with us for many years and had a stroke and died while she was being cared for in a home for a few days so that mother and father could have a short holiday. After she died, so did the room, losing its identity in a growing muddle of unwanted things sitting awkwardly, and sometimes grotesquely, side by side. On one of my last visits, when father was no longer making much sense of the world, I pulled open the bureau lid again and found inside a plate with two sandwiches covered in blue mould.

THE SHED

A mini-home in itself, a room in which to hide in the time-honoured fashion of husbands, the shed appeared on the site of the air-raid shelter just a few years before father's retirement. First, some men came and poured concrete to make a foundation (at long last father had a motive for cutting the long grass), then they came back another day and erected the wooden construction, under father's severe draughtsman's eye.

There it stood: four wooden walls, door, sloping roof and little window; innocuous in appearance, a source of continual exasperation to mother. For one thing, she resented his locking it, although it was reasonable enough, being near the back gate, which was always open. Perhaps it was the fact that he didn't put the key on a hook in the kitchen as he did with other keys, but kept it himself, slipping it into his pocket, not looking her in the face if she was present. What could she say? She would have no reason to go in there, among nails and hammers, would she?

Bit by bit he fitted it out, making bus trips to the ironmonger's and the new DIY centre. Money was not so tight now that the house was just for the two of them and me, and soon I would leave school and have a grant, courtesy of Mr. Wilson, which father would just have to top up. So he indulged himself, at last, in a hobby. One of the first things that came out of that shed was the rose trellis, beneath which he photographed mother sitting at her ease, so she really should not have been full of resentment, yet she was. She wanted him to help his son out - unemployment, by then, was becoming a permanent condition for many people, especially as they got older - and spending money on a hobby seemed to her totally unjustified.

"I'm not giving him money to go and squander in pubs", was his reply.

The little shed, in the sound of its hammer blows, drove itself between them inch by inch. Sometimes she would go down, still in her apron, to the shed door on some pretext, say "Dinner'll be ready in ten minutes" (as if he didn't know what time dinner always was) and stand at the door peering in, but never, never, did she put a foot inside.

In my last year of school, a year of relative freedom in which I could organize my schoolwork more or less as I thought best, I was given the chance to paint a large picture, bigger than I had ever handled before, to be hung in the entrance hall. I was given the measurements, but I would have to prepare the board, or the canvas, myself and take it to the school.

I stepped into the shed. Father was rubbing a piece of wood with sandpaper, his glasses on the end of his nose, his pursed-up mouth blowing the dust away. He was in his shirt-sleeves, but he had not taken off his tie. It was the first time I had been properly inside his den. As was to be expected, there wasn't a nail out of place: on the shelves, plastic boxes were lined up, each one meticulously labelled - screws, tacks, nails, hooks, tape - and from hooks in the walls files, chisels, squares and hammers hung in sets, arranged by size from largest to smallest. The work bench was swept clean, and even the shavings on the floor were all gathered in one place.

As if it was all not really for making, but rather for being.

When he knew what was wanted, nothing was too much trouble. We did not have a car, but in some way unknown to me he got a large sheet of hardboard brought home and set about framing it. After that it had to be painted white, which I wanted to do myself. One of the things I had learnt was that the ground to be painted on should have what the teacher called 'tooth' ("tuth", he said in the southern way, so that at first I had not understood) and this could be obtained on smooth hardboard by laying on the paint in various directions.

When father saw me doing this he took the brush from my hand.

"That's no way to go about it. You want to go up and down, and back and forth, look, like this."

"It's not a *wall*," I said crossly, pitying him his ignorance.

He took the whole thing out of my hands, planing the edges, whitewashing it in his own fashion, until I wondered if he wanted to paint a picture on it himself. By the time we took it - in a neighbour's van - to the school art room, I wished him elsewhere. How strange and embarrassing to see my father in school, and in the one place I always thought of as my haven that gave me glimpses of another world to be lived in! As I watched him manoeuvring the board with the aid of the teacher, uneasy and awkward in this new situation, I felt his presence as a contamination of something that was precious to me, and I was glad to see him go.

After the rose trellis, my board and one or two little shelves, nothing came out of the shed, but father continued to spend time in it, apparently always finding things to plane and sandpaper, but never things that later appeared in the house.

It was my last summer at home. I had already cried my heart out, in secret, for the loss of school, but the prospect of an unknown place all yet to be discovered (far away!) and every day in which to do the things I loved doing, were beginning to stir my fantasy. I could see that life was becoming, as in *Alice*, a corridor full of doors you could open or not. It was our last time together and we tiptoed through it, being gentle with one another, damping down potential arguments so as not to spoil it.

I was with mother in the kitchen when Ken arrived, and it was apparent right away that he was in a positive mood, giving us a bright smile and his routine "All right then,

Mam?" Getting the cups out of the cabinet, she was reminded that one of the metal arms holding the drop-down worktop was coming loose.

"Just look here, I'm afraid of this coming down on my feet. I've told your father a dozen times. Can you have a look at it?"

He peered. "Nothing to it. Got a screwdriver?"

"They're all in your dad's shed."

Father had been pottering in his shed until half an hour before, and when he left to go and buy something he said he needed right away, he had not locked it as he usually did. The key, in fact, was hanging in the lock on the outside.

I could see, by the way father walked up the path, that he had seen evidence of someone having been in his shed while he was out. His mouth was set. The cabinet was fully functional again; Ken stood with the screwdriver and pliers in his hand; mother stood with the tea caddy in hers; father stepped over the threshold and before he could speak she said,

"Ken's just fixed the cabinet for me, look…"

"I can see that. Just see you put them right back where you got them from. And *ask* next time."

Tea was not drunk. Ken walked off down the path, his back very straight and his hands in his trouser pockets, and slammed shut the gate. Whenever I think of him, that is one picture that always rises before me: there he is, walking away down the path alone, hands in pockets, forever walking away.

THE HALL

A place on the way to somewhere, a narrow place with very little light where you did not stop for long, nor did you sit down. There were two chairs in the hall, but only because there was nowhere else to put them when they were not being sat upon during Sunday lunches.

Most of the hall was taken up by a massive wardrobe, a vast Victorian piece that belonged to my grandmother and remained with us after she died. It had a mirror on the door, and when I pulled it open by the little round brass handle, it made a sound like in a horror film when you know you are going to see something terrible. Inside there was a musty smell and yellow brittle pages of newspaper on the bottom. After Nanna died, nothing much was kept in there, just a few rain clothes and umbrellas and anything about which mother could say, "There's nowhere for this thing to go."

Behind the wardrobe we trod the narrow staircase with its zigzag carpet that covered only the centre of each stair, where you put your feet, and left the sides bare to collect dust and fluff. I learned that the third stair was the one that creaked, the one to avoid if you wanted to listen without being seen, which I sometimes did.

Sitting in my pyjamas, I peered behind the top of the wardrobe from where I could see the door of the living room, left ajar. Through the gap a piece of my mother occasionally flashed by, accompanied by her exclamations:

"Oh *YOU!* It's impossible to talk to you!"

Followed by an odd kind of gasping and shuffling. An arm was flung out. My father's voice came harsh but quavering.

"At least I don't spend it all down at the pub every night!

And once, I paused on my way down and caught my grandmother with the door of her room open, murmuring to herself, "Eh, well, perhaps he'll go soon, some of 'em do go at fifty."

My cold indifference to her dated from that evening.

At the bottom of the stairs there was a small frosted window with some tiny coloured glass decoration in the centre of it and below the window ledge, a three-sided cupboard on which I kept, for a very few months, my cage of white mice until they died – of starvation or boredom – and I buried them with all due ceremony and crosses in the back garden, inducing mother's sentimental tears. In a later period, some poor goldfish circulated in a bowl on the window ledge and ended up in the same cemetery in a very short time. I took these deaths with solemnity and wonder, but did not then connect them with my inability to provide the proper nurturing care.

After that, for many years two other objects stood on the window ledge and on the cupboard, out there in the hall, in the shadows, as if mother were trying to keep them hidden and safe. One was a small silver-plated cup mounted on a plastic base. On the base, in capital letters, were the words *Royal Oak Darts Team* and below that, in gilt script the words *All the Best Ken*. When I first saw that cup I had already become a visitor to the house, my life was taking place elsewhere and I had not seen my brother for many years, so when it caught my eye just as I was swinging around to place my foot on the first stair, I paused and took it up and read it. It said so very much. Above all, it said that he was good at something, good enough to win. It said that others appreciated him for this, and in those simple final words devoid of all spurious formality it said that others knew how much he suffered and wished him a better life. He had brought it here, to her, because there was, then, between marriages, nowhere else he could take it, and she had placed it there with pride. But it came from the pub, and that was enough for father to pass it over as if it were nothing, to make it impossible for mother to stand it on the mantelpiece in the living-room.

The other object, occupying the place of my mice, had been there for much longer, and it was a small wooden box, three-sided like the cupboard it stood on. Ken had brought it home from school one day and it said, like the cup: *look what I can do.* Woodwork was the only subject that didn't frighten him because he could do it without having to speak. He stumbled over words but his fingers didn't stumble over the wood, they moved with certainty like a pianist over the keys, searching for perfection. So, when he got into the Woodwork Room (which must have been like the Art Room for me in my school - large windows, full of only apparent chaos and open spaces that invited movement instead of rows of desks that ordered you to be still) he moved with confidence, knowing what he was doing, and nobody asked him to say anything if he didn't want.

He had made a little three-sided box to fit in a corner, with a little door that opened onto two small shelves. The whole thing was meticulously finished, the edges rounded off, the joints flush, everything varnished and polished three times over. The little knob on the door had been particularly difficult to turn, you could see that. Now it stood on the living-room table, exposed like a chicken out of the egg.

When I came close, in my myopic fashion, he pushed my hands away.

"*Gerroff*! It's not for *you*!"

Of course, it was for her. Mother took hold of the little knob and pulled the door, which opened with a slight tacky sound, it was so new and fresh. Peering in at the two clean shelves she exclaimed:

"Ooh, isn't that nice!"

He hung around, silent, on a little cloud of pleasure.

"And did you do all that by yourself? Isn't it lovely!" she went on.

When father came home in the evening, the box had to come out again – there it was on the table among the tea things.

"Look what he's made me, isn't it good? He's done it all on his own, you know, there in Woodwork."

"Has he now? Well, let's have a look, then."

Father adjusted his glasses. All of a sudden, the little box ceased to be a pleasure and became an exam. You could feel the change in the air. Ken looked away, seemingly indifferent. Mother wiped her hands on her apron and fiddled with the teacups. I waited and watched. Father gave the box a thorough going-over, scrutinising every angle, line and joint. At last:

"Mmm. Very nice. Not bad at all, that."

And just as his son began to turn towards him like a plant towards the light, he added:

"Now let's see if you can't get your Maths and English up to the same standard."

A small silence, everything spiralling down, then mother gathered up the box.

"Well, I'm thrilled to bits with it, it's just the thing for my cottons" she said, and she swept it out away from father as one must shield certain flowering plants from the powerful sun, which does not strengthen their growth but only ruins the blooms. The box found its place in the hall, alongside the trophy.

The hall was where post fell onto the mat and the evening paper was delivered, besides magazines that got stuck in the flap: *Woman's Own, Girl's Friend, The Dandy, The Beano, The Eagle, Bunty.* There was hardly a day when something to read didn't arrive. Each of us received our instructions, in simple, illustrated terms, for living: mother learned how to keep her family happy and healthy, how to fill any spare moments she might have with little extras for others' comfort; Doreen and Ida learned the best ways to catch a husband, how to match shoes and bags, tips on applying make-up; Ken learned… what did he learn?

Now and then, when I'd finished mine, I used to read his comics if he wasn't around. How different they were! The drawings were different to start with, more dramatic, strange perspectives and the dialogue bubbles were full of exclamations: *I'll show them! You won't get away with this! We'll never make it in time! Aaaaagh!* The characters were mainly men or monsters, if there were girls they were tearful and had to be rescued, and they always were. The others were divided into Goodies and Baddies, and the Goodies always won. They had strong jaws and muscular arms and sometimes flew or walked up sides of buildings, or transformed themselves entirely into something else.

My own comics were not like that. The girls in the stories physically resembled more or less all the girls around me, even down to the school uniforms. There was the one with perfect hair and long lashes, the sensible, organising one and the one with plaits, wide-eyed, who believed everything she heard. They did the same things we did, they loved kittens and puppies and ballet and they never flew or saved anybody or did anything dangerous. Sometimes the comic contained a free necklace or a ring. My comics were the run-up to my sisters' magazines, but by the time I was out of them I was safe from *Woman's Own* because the Sixties were ushering in alternatives - there was sometimes a girl in the stories who was not like the others, a 'bit of a tomboy' as mother would put it - and I was beginning to get a glimpse of a woman's life that might contain something more than a husband and a house.

All the magazines that came into the house lay around for some days after they were read, and all of them passed through my hands. There was a time, in that brief scary space which is the end of childhood and the beginning of not being a child, in which it became my habit, when I was sitting in an armchair, to take a pen and one of the old magazines and to draw tears on all the faces I could find.

"Look what she does. Why do you make everyone cry?"

I had no answer to give.

Eventually, at eighteen, I walked down that hall and out of that door forever. The last to fly the nest, I had chosen a place to study that was far away, and I packed my two little cases with an indifference that only youth can flaunt. I have no memory of that last night – what was done, what might have been said – only one thing remains crystallised in a frame throughout all the years of my life, remaining in my heart like a sharp fragment: me sitting in a taxi with father, and mother standing small upon the doorstep, weeping, her apron going up to her eyes while I give a perfunctory careless little wave before turning my face aside from her.

So began the search for Home. People call this search by other names: freedom, adventure, experience, opportunity. Mother called it *Gadding About*. Once, people didn't *gad about*, they moved up the street or into the next town and only to the other end of the country if they were compelled, but not by choice. I saw how incomprehensible my behaviour was to her, an aberration, unnatural, unfeminine. Home is where we start from and often we seem to be further and further away from what we need although we know for sure that it is not behind us. Home must be where we are, it has to be, because if we are here and Home is elsewhere, there is no peace.

The hall was also the place of bad news: police officers in uniform and behind them, the blue light flashing in the darkness.

Drunk and disorderly.

Breaking open the meter.

Overdose.

A missing handbag.

Overdose.

Ken married again, but before he found Belle there was

nothing much for him but continuous unemployment, pub life and above all, the desolate domestic life of a single man who does not know how to transform the bare walls and ugly furniture of other people's houses into something you can call home. Often it takes very little - a couple of pictures, some bright comfortable cushions, a plant - but males on their own, especially if their hearts are breaking, need much more than that. Women hang on by a thread sometimes and from that tenuous thread, when the world has stopped shaking, they can weave a whole new existence, but the male will not believe in a thread. The solitary male, to escape from his bleak bedsitter, goes to the pub and sometimes drinks too much. If there was no work there was dole money at least, and if that ran out there was a way of breaking open the meter to fish out the shillings, and if you couldn't do that you could get hold of a magnet that stopped the thing from turning so you didn't have to put any more money in. These were the first things that brought the flashing blue light to our door, that enraged father and embarrassed my respectably married sisters (what will the neighbours think!). There was even the notoriety of a little piece in the local newspaper, after a particularly rowdy evening at the pub. ' *"I'll Kill Him" Shout by Youth*': Ida showed mother the paper, flapping it with indignation, and mother read it out loud, her hand on her chest.

"Oh, my goodness me!"

Soon after that, with still no light on the horizon, he opened the first bottle of pills, which was enough to get him into the emergency room but not enough to do the trick. But escape by the chemical path had been opened to him and in those days, in a post-industrial city living on its former glories and little else, it was not difficult to inject yourself into a better frame of mind for a few hours.

It was in the pub that he met Belle. She was a few years older than him, plump and sensible-faced, and they had divorce in common to begin with. Things were looking up; they married, she gave him two children, a dark-eyed girl in his own image and a fair boy with his father's wide smile, something not seen for so very long. All this came to me through letters only, in mother's conversational script:

They seem to be hitting it off together, I do hope so.

Belle and Ken came for tea, she's such a nice girl.

On one of my ever rarer visits home, I decided to go and see for myself. I was a little worried about my reception; I had not seen my brother for so long and, as there were still no phones at either end, I was going unannounced. But mother had said "He often asks about you", and that was enough.

In the early afternoon I took the bus into that part of the town which was almost unknown to me, where I had gone with mother to the mean little house with nothing in the cupboard, where the shops were shabbier, the roads littered and gardens almost non-existent. Checking my paper with the address, I sought out the right number in a street of terraced houses with bay windows. Some were brightly painted, with flowers in the minuscule front garden; others had grey windows and rubbish stacked outside. The house I came to was neat and tidy. A child's bicycle leant against the inside of the low wall. When I rang the bell, there was a running of feet and a child's voice inside, and after a minute the door was opened by a woman with curly brown hair and a face red from some physical effort I had just interrupted. She had a towel in her hand. When she knew who I was she seemed astonished at first and then, turning inside, she invited me into the hall, calling out at the same time,

"Ken! It's your sister!"

We manoeuvred past the big pram standing in the hallway, which was even narrower than ours at home, and over her shoulder I saw through an open door a dimly-lit sitting room where a little girl of about five was dancing around between the television and her father. When she saw me she stopped, stared at me with her father's dark eyes and put her hands on her head. Ken was sitting on a sofa rolling a cigarette. Just a few years had bared his temples, the Elvis quiff a far-off memory, his cheekbones were too pronounced and the indoor pallor of his skin made me suddenly ashamed of my own healthy tan, betraying me as one who had got away. He did not get up, but gave me a fleeting glance and a brief, sardonic smile and said hello before returning to his delicate task.

Belle turned down the volume of the television and stood close by, waiting for something that she thought should happen, and I could tell she was disappointed, as though my arrival were to have been some kind of medicine that would restore her husband to vitality.

"I'll make some tea, you'll have some, won't you?"

She left us for a few moments, and I did not know what to say to my brother. He gave me no handles, just concentrating on his cigarette paper with a scientific precision that was his father's, had he but been aware of it. To my banal domestic enquiries he returned a yes (he liked the house all right) or no (he didn't have a job) or a lift of the shoulders (his daughter was the image of him). I said nothing about my own life and he asked nothing. The muted TV programme flickered and a budgie tweeted in a cage hanging outside the window. The little girl was a flame of pure life, dancing away there in the middle of the little room, chattering to herself, flicking back her long black hair. As children do, she was pretending to take no notice of us, but all her efforts were aimed at flirting with her father, and suddenly, without a word, she ran to him and flung her arms around his neck. Then he laid his cigarette carefully aside and embraced her; totally, unsparingly. They remained like that in silence.

How he loves her. See how he loves her.

Belle returned with a little baby boy in her arms ("just woken up") and there they all were, a family. But he sat there with something that kept him in darkness, as if he were sitting at the bottom of a well and could neither climb out by his own efforts nor be pulled out by someone as willing and loving as his wife and daughter.

After tea, I got up to leave, and it was at that point that he roused himself. I thanked Belle at the door, but Ken came with me to the gate and when it closed between us - me on the outside, him on the inside - and I said goodbye, I looked into his face and saw that there were tears in his eyes. All the things not said in the previous hour were there, dumb and dangerous. With his hand on the gate he watched me as I walked away.

There came, eventually, a letter in father's hand. This was such an unusual event I knew something must be wrong, but I had to forage between the lines and they were very few:

We have had a nice week at Llandudno. Weather not too bad. Mum was pleased though. She has been a bit upset lately with Ken's behaviour...

That year, I changed jobs and country, but before leaving I went home for two or three days to say, once again, goodbye to them. It was then that I saw they were getting old: the blue veins in father's cold cheek, his skull outlined beneath the sparse white hair, the way he bent to throw something in the fireplace. And mother - look at her, here in the bedroom talking to me before sleep.

Mother does not believe she is old, she will never believe it. Her Crimplene frock, her pink underskirt; sticking out her tongue with the effort, she unfastens the clips on her corsets, and her belly, freed and safely hidden behind closed curtains, settles comfortably where it wanted to be. She was never a fat woman; I have her small bones and stature. She stands in her long vest and all her body, from the lines on her temples to the skin between her toes, all her flesh is falling, yearning towards the earth. She is tired, her white breast that has never seen the sun is tired, lying wrinkled in her vest, but her legs, bruised and veined as they are, stand firmly planted on the rug like two slim marble columns. Once again, I am suddenly ashamed of my tanned, untried flesh that I have been so vain about lately. This is my mother, this woman's flesh has generated all of us, amazingly, wonderfully.

She talks quietly, a little to me, a little to herself.

"Let me put my cream on. I like to keep my skin nice, even if I am getting on a bit. Well, we all do, don't we?"

No, she does not really believe she is getting old. Perhaps it is simply willpower that keeps her hair not-quite grey, although she and father are the same age; her heart going like a train; her eyes bright and her legs nimble, running about chicken-like all day long. Once a week she puts on her coat and hat and while father goes off to the library for his books about the age of the great ships, she goes off to the town centre where the price of a coffee will give her a morning's chat with her friend Winnie and even - precious thing! - laughter. Now she stands rubbing the cream on her face and neck, observing herself curiously in the mirror, gestures of a young girl that never leave us. Rubbing cream into tired white flesh and all the scars are on the inside, but it is the best you can do, I think as I watch her, sitting on her bed. I am one of those scars, I know I am, it is the wound I inflicted when I left. I did not know that there would be a corresponding scar on my side.

"Goodnight, then."

"Goodnight, my love. Sleep tight."

The next morning, which was my last day, I sat in the living-room going through my bag and checking over my documents and money for my trip, while father was out for bread and mother was making the beds. A one-way ticket, a passport, the letters concerning my job and a couple of hundred pounds to fill the gap before my first pay. I decided to check it and began to count out the notes on the arm of the chair.

The house was silent, the only sound was the faint crackling from the small fire in the grate. A hundred and sixty, seventy, eighty... I came to the end and squared up the pile on the arm of the chair, raising my glance to the window in front of me as I did so.

Why did my blood run so cold? It was only my own brother standing there, not a bogeyman. I had not heard the latch on the gate nor his footsteps on the path, and instead of opening the back door he had come to the window – why did he do that? – and was looking down at the money in my hands. When he raised his eyes to mine he gave a broad smile like the ones in the early holiday photographs, a smile that was like the sun coming out, that I had not seen for so long and which gave no warning of disaster.

Mother had seen him from the upstairs window and came

downstairs to make tea. Not long after, father came home with the bread and we all seemed to hover between the kitchen, the hall and the living-room, with nobody sitting down except me. There was a tension in the air and it seemed to me that the simple things that were said - the weather, the tea, the traffic - were taking the place of other, vital things that were not said, and never would be. Mother in particular kept looking about her nervously.

The moment came in which father was upstairs in the bedroom changing his shoes, I was in the bathroom and mother was paying the window cleaner, who had called with his bill, and when I came down again my brother and my bag were gone.

As I have said, I am calm in a storm. Already in my mind I was going over the material consequences of not flying the next day, not starting my job on time and losing the only spare money I had just then. Mother was distraught, but not surprised - that was why she had been so nervous.

"It's not the first time. He's been in my bag more than once."

Father was beside himself. He stood in the doorway, frustrated with helplessness, and seemed to swell inside his clothes. The loose skin on his cheeks shook as he spat out the words:

"That's it! I've finished with him now!"

We decided, father and I, to go out and look for him. He was on foot, at the most he could have taken a bus into the town, and on this hopeless supposition we set out. It was better than doing nothing. From a phone box father dialled 999 and reported his son for theft. After tramping uselessly round a few streets chosen at random, father got an asthma attack and we had to go home, where he could grab his inhaler. There was no comfort for anyone and little we could do to help one another - most of the afternoon passed in this limbo and then came the flashing blue light in the hall again and a policeman stood there with my small brown bag in his hand. They had not 'caught' him; he had gone to them himself, after leaving the bag in the park, where they had gone to pick it up and bring it to me. Everything was still in it; he had spent just five pounds. (Probably on drink, muttered father.)

I sat in the police station room while the officer wrote down his report, sitting opposite me. It was very quiet all around and the brown-furnished room was dimly lit, creating an atmosphere that was strangely, domestically, cosy. He got to a certain point in the account and then looked up from his paper.

"You can press charges, you know, if you want to."

Charges, against my own brother.

"No, I don't want to do that."

"Sure?"

"Yes, it doesn't matter."

He went away and came back and wrote for a few moments and while I sat there waiting for him to finish, I noticed behind his back a movement along the corridor. The window of the room was merely a high strip of glass so that I could only see the head and shoulders of whoever passed, but it was enough space and enough time to see that a policeman was escorting a man, my brother, to the exit. How strange that seemed, as if he was just anybody in the hands of the police, as if we had nothing to do with each other. By the time I left, he had vanished.

The next morning, I got up very early and left for the airport. They stood together in the hallway and watched me go, his hand on her shoulder, as in the painting I have made of them, seeming so small, so defenceless against the blows.

Father even asked me what to do once, about my brother, and I fled from it, as if he was trying to heave a sack of coal onto my shoulders as the Coal Men used to do outside the gate.

"He's asked me for twenty pounds."

I looked away.

"What shall I do? Shall I give it him?"

He seemed small and vulnerable, so afraid of doing the wrong thing.

"I don't know."

"Your mother thinks I should, of course." Perhaps he was even more afraid of displeasing her.

Father's shirts disappeared from the wardrobe, money from mother's bag, a heavy winter coat. He never had enough money. The last time I saw him was unplanned, as was my own visit to them. Where there was no telephone, surprise arrivals were the norm, warnings given by letter did not always arrive on time, sometimes were deliberately not given.

Mother saw him first as she stood at the sink and called from the kitchen, her tone a mixture of fear and joy.

"Here's Ken!"

Father remained in his armchair and I felt, once again, as if I were at the theatre waiting for the act to begin. If I had been able, I would have hidden behind the Girls' Annual as I did so long ago.

My brother appeared at the living room door, holding on to the doorknob but not coming right in, so that only one side of his body and his head were visible. He was wearing a dark raincoat, too thin for the cold weather.

I was shocked. Was he so old? Had it been so long? He had already lost most of his hair and his mouth was pulled tightly down like that of an old man in constant pain. His lovely eyes, those dark, long-lashed eyes that had always smiled before his mouth smiled, were spent and his look was – the words leapt to my mind – that of a beaten dog. I was so shocked I could say nothing but a tiny hello, the bag episode floating between us like contaminated air. But he was barely aware of me. He continued to stand there, half in and half out of the room, his gaze fixed on his father, who remained in his armchair and would not meet his eye. Mother, out in the hallway, kept asking him to come in properly, to have something to eat, and he went on refusing; no, he had to go somewhere, he had to see someone... but he never took his eyes off his father; waiting, waiting....

Then he was gone.

The worst visit of all she had to bear alone in the end, father being gone by then into his private personal world and no longer able to live with her. So all alone she had to get up from her armchair, walk down the hall in her slippers, open the door, see the flashing light – why is it always night? – and know that, two hundred miles away in another city, her son was winding down his life in a hospital bed and that only when they had made him understand that there was no possibility of winding it up again, that the poison he had filled his vein with this time – knowingly or unknowingly was never to be established – was consuming all of him, only then did he stop denying that he had a family – not even Belle and his children – and give *her* name and address. There was still no phone in the house, not even in the Eighties, so the policewoman in her neat blue uniform had to go and raise the door knocker and tell mother, when she opened the door a tiny crack, that the story was coming to an end.

After the funeral, mother went upstairs even before she had taken off her coat, went in a great hurry, as though she had been thinking of it all through the service in the draughty side chapel where those who dare to take God's life out of themselves are committed to the flames; she went upstairs and brought down to us, all arranged stuffily in the little living-room once again, a large, framed sepia-coloured photograph which I had never known was in the house. It was a picture of a fine-looking young man with dark wavy hair, gazing steadily into the distance away from the camera.

"Look," she said to us, standing in the middle of the room in her coat, with her hat knocked crooked from the effort of searching in some upstairs cupboard. "Look, you'd think it was him, wouldn't you? But it's his dad. Aren't they alike?"

I realised I was looking at a photograph of my father in his youth and strength. Everybody seemed to have been made embarrassed and uncomfortable by her gesture, as if they could not cope with it. They started busying themselves arranging on the table the cold food that nobody really wanted to eat, but she remained there with the picture in her hands, oblivious to us all. Look, *look*.

"The very image."

She went on gazing, turning the glass this way and that to see better, and in her face there was an agonised confusion.

THE BIG ROOM

When I rang the bell, the nurse who opened it looked surprised. Do so few people come here? I gave my father's name and she opened the door a bit wider to let me in, standing aside in her pale blue overall. Then off up the corridor she went, walking briskly into a big room, and I followed through the ranks of slippers and stained cardigans and toothless jaws. Into the big light room we went and I looked hard to find him, because they all seemed to be similar, like variations on a theme: *dementia senex*. The tall windows, without curtains, threw light in abundance into the middle of the floor but the men were all arranged in chairs against the walls. The chairs in such places always look uncomfortable, with their wooden arms and thin backs, without cushions, as if people who are losing control of their minds do not need soft comfort. The walls behind them were green to just above their heads and then an indefinite shade of beige up to the ceiling, which was very high. There were two or three tables, one with a folded newspaper on it, the others bare, but no cupboards or shelves. One solitary bad landscape painting was hung on one wall. Some of the men were asleep, leaning to one side in their chairs; some were conversing with their demons; others were staring ahead of them. It seemed like a station waiting room in a bad dream.

When I did spot him it seemed absurd to me that I could possibly have confused him with anyone else, despite his shrunken frame.

"You've got a visitor, Alfred".

I was momentarily shocked by the use of his first name, as if the nurse had known him all her life. He belonged here now, he belonged to these people.

He sat with his arms laid along the arms of the chair and his feet together, gazing across the room. He had the regulation tartan slippers they all had, a baggy pair of grey trousers and a beige cardigan a bit stained down the front. His tie was still knotted carefully at his throat. There was a second when he looked at me and I was nothing to him, and I thought I would die if it went on, but then his filing cabinet of memory, which had been ransacked by an intruder and everything thrown up into the air to settle again any old how, still managed to come up with the right reference, and he smiled; his tongue leaping about like an oyster in its toothless cavern, he smiled at me and his watery eyes wrinkled up, his glasses gone now. As a child I had always been alarmed when he took off his glasses - those bushy brows! They were grey now but still had the same power to alarm when they shot up: at the nurse who withholds the biscuit; at the brisk young fool of a doctor; at the idiot in the next chair.

He held my hand and laughed a lot. I had never seen him laugh so much; this new world seemed a great joke. He pointed to a button on his cardigan.

"Look at that," murmured the mathematician, running his finger round the edge of it. "It's perfect."

Together we bent our heads and contemplated the satisfaction of a perfect circle.

Oh, I remember you: the one who cut his food into precise pieces before eating, who had to have the tablecloth square on; who went to bed like a letter going into an envelope; who paid the bills the day after they came, keeping careful accounts of so little; a man walking on a tightrope, fearful lest he should drop it all into the abyss and go hurtling after. "Ask your father, he'll know, he'll decide." But there was a wild untended place in the garden, and I woke in the night and *Dear God* he was sobbing, *help me.*

At first, mother had come a few times, refusing to recognize that this was no ordinary spell in hospital, bringing receipts of bills for him to see, holding them under his nose.

"There, I've paid that then Alfred, see?"

He would not look at them but gazed into the distance, infuriating her because it was so unlike him. He had forgotten how to read, in any case; words had become once again just black marks on paper, as they were in the very beginning. He was unlearning all his skills: reading forgotten, and the use of a fork getting more difficult day by day; soon he would unlearn how to walk; shedding all the accumulated skins of being grown-up, he was retreating down a long dark tunnel, smaller and simpler he was becoming, laughing and waving, free at last.

A nurse in a green overall was urging somebody across the room, her voice bright and brisk:

"Just follow your stick, George!"

George passed us by, a powerful smell of urine about him. He was wearing faded pyjamas, those old-fashioned blue and white striped pyjamas that my father had worn, with the drawstring waist. In his haste to get to the bathroom they were coming undone, his withered old sex trembling in the shadow. I wondered if George had anything to ask forgiveness for, if he had ever been heard weeping in the night.

The only journey I had ever made with my father, as an adult, was the one that took me away from home for the first time, the one that began with leaving mother crying into her apron on the doorstep. In the echoing main-line station I stood with my luggage - the least I have had in my life - while father queued up to buy tickets. There was a long queue and I spent the time looking around at the people coming and going, thinking that I was about to become one of them, and when I glanced back at the queue to find out how much progress he had made, I could not find my father. For a moment I felt a slight panic, thinking he had changed queue and not told me, but then I recognised him. I had not seen him immediately because I had been looking for a tall man and my father was the shortest man in the queue.

Look. My father is a small man.

It was a four-hour journey down to London and I cannot remember any kind of conversation between us. He left me at my lodging, walking away to the bus stop with straight shoulders and high head as if it didn't matter, but I knew, I knew. He had kept all my school reports. That last summer, before I left home, he did nothing but take photographs of me. Once I found him furtively copying out the address of a boyfriend I had. Once I had even wished him dead.

I looked down at my hand holding my father's hand. They were both cold, they might have been a marble sculpture. He does not know. Nobody can tell him, and perhaps he would not even understand it now if they did.

I looked at an old man who was sitting opposite us, nodding and chuckling, his open mouth showing a few brown stubs of teeth. He seemed like an evil dwarf laughing at us.

George's head was bent between thin cardiganed shoulders. His elbows were stuck out to steady him and his free hand shook the air in front of him as if testing for invisible obstacles. His baggy pyjama trousers wrinkled up over the slippers, too big, that splayed out to left and right as he made his lonely, inch-by-inch journey across the floor to the toilets. No crossing of continents or oceans was ever such an achievement.

I looked around me. It was the only time I had ever been in a room where there were so many men present but so little sense of power in the air. So - this was Man, made in the image of God, shuffling in a stained cardigan and flapping slippers along the corridor, spittle brimming on a slack lip.

THE LAST ROOM

I wondered at first whether I would be able to find it. I thought I knew, in my memory, the lie of the land once outside the station, but to my surprise the streets turned differently from the way I remembered them. I set off walking towards the town and within five minutes saw, to my right, a long tree-lined avenue that had lain forgotten in my memory for decades, but now leapt to the foreground, opening a floodgate: this was the Art Gallery, the very first of many in my life, the place where I had spent so many Saturday afternoons alone, peering into other worlds and finding out how all this magic was done. The sudden joy I felt on seeing its dome at the end of the avenue was not in keeping with my reason for being there, and although I would have loved to go in and see all the pictures again - I knew nearly all of them intimately and I thought how they had remained there, immobile, gazing out all those years - I pressed on up the slope towards the town centre.

My journey had begun far away, the previous evening, and taking the train from south to north I had had to change at a major junction. Millions of people have changed trains in this station since its grand opening in the mid-nineteenth century, hauling their lives and luggage north, south, east and west. Wandering about the platform searching for places sheltered from the wind, it came upon me suddenly that this was the very station where, one month after his fortieth birthday, Ken had collapsed and been gathered up by strangers and taken away. Stations change, get modernised: new floors, glass plating, new offices, modern waiting rooms, monitors, flowerbeds... but the old Victorian structures remain: the robust lamp-posts, the wrought iron, the warm-coloured, thick brick walls with gothic windows. I laid my hand on the limestone brick window sill and thought that he might have done the same twenty years before, laid his hand right here, when he felt himself falling.

It was an autumn day of raggedy trees, a high wind and that astonishing bright blue sky that you can occasionally get before winter sets in, everything sharp and clear, almost hurting the eyes. The wind pushed against me all the way up the road; not much traffic, a few little shops on either side, once thriving, now some of them boarded up forever, and then - too soon, I was not ready yet - I came across the sign, there between a baker's and a bank.

Fenton Funeral Services.

It had always been there, that sign, but was never one of

the shops we went into, there was nothing in the window, it was nothing to do with us, it was just there. The area had become a pedestrian zone and there was a bench a little way off, under a young scraggy tree that was shedding its last leaves, and at the same time as I thought about going and sitting for a while, my hand was pushing open the door and I went straight in. At the desk the young woman dressed in a dark suit smiled, like a receptionist in a hotel. She had been reading a magazine.

"I've come to see my mother."

Unreal, absurd words.

"Name? Just a moment please."

Then she went off along a small corridor and came back after a few minutes, gesturing to me to go with her. I walked behind her between dark wooden walls without windows or pictures and just one dim light in the ceiling.

There was a sliding door, one of several, where she stopped and said, still smiling:

"Stay as long as you like."

Her heels retreated back to the magazine and I was suddenly left alone in a tiny brown cubicle, dimly lit by a wall lamp. There were two chairs and a table with the coffin on it. The coffin was open, the lid leaning against the wall, and I realised that that was what the receptionist had done in the minutes when she came alone before me, she had taken off the lid and laid it there. I read the name and the dates and the completion of it, the finality, came home to me. It was then that I saw that the tiny room had no window: who would have been looking out?

I lowered myself carefully onto a chair; in the dim glow of the lamp reflected in the polished wood and the absolute silence it seemed as if I were waiting for something to begin, for the curtain to rise, the music to strike up, the show to commence. From where I was sitting I could not see into the coffin; only a tuft of grey hair and the tip of her nose were visible. I sat very still and waited.

"Mummy," I said, looking up. It was all looking up then, when you were the smallest. "Mummy, I don't want you to die." I had seen a film. They all laughed then. Kids, the things they say. "Don't you, lovey? Well, I don't want to die either, and I'm not going to, not for a very long time."

The very long time has run out, and now I am looking down.

They did not want her to die alone in a crumbling house; that's why they swept her up, with a few belongings, into a flat in sheltered housing. I know that they thought it was right, I know that they were in good faith, that being so far away from it I could not reasonably have expected to have a say in the matter, but oh, would it have mattered so much, the dirty floors, the crumbling woodwork, the wild garden, if she could have stayed among her memories until the very end of fifty years? We are not supposed to cling to the things of this world, but sometimes these *things*, these smallnesses, are so imbued with history, with meaning for us - that door, that window, *that* mantelpiece and no other – that to tear them away from us is a wound to the spirit.

They had let her take her couch and armchair, the TV, the living-room table, her bed and all her kitchen and bathroom things. A thousand small, precious things had been thrown away in black plastic bags, a handful salvaged; the glory hole and its contents were abandoned; the piano, nanna's wardrobe and the bureau were sold; the grass crept up to the dusty windows.

The first day, she disappeared from the residence and caused a general panic, which only ceased when she returned in the late afternoon, marvelling at the fuss. She had been, she said, to *look at the house*. I do not know if she ever did it again. When I visited her in the flat for the first time, I took down the photograph album from a built-in cupboard where they had put it away, while she busied herself with tea things. I made it seem as if I were casually turning over the pages but really I wanted to find some pictures of my brother and maybe ask for one to take away. When I came to those pages where I knew they should have been, they were all empty, the little triangles framing nothing. As I looked up at her, about to speak, she moved off into the kitchen. She must have thrown them all away. For an instant I was angered and shocked at this gesture; for an instant only, then I realised that it was not what it seemed but indeed the opposite: the only way she could coax her heart to go on beating.

Now I sat up straighter, I could see more, and for a moment I thought that those eyes were going to snap open suddenly and turn that brown stare on me again.

"Oh, you're a Little madam! Never do anything you're told!"

Then I bent forward, looked more closely and saw that the closed eyes were different; something beneath the lids was gone and the silence was not the silence of a sleeper but the silence of forever which will never be broken.

She's not here, she's not here... and the dream came to my mind again. I was searching desperately all the rooms of the house for her, so that panic swept in for a moment and beat its wings against the walls of the windowless room, but then my fingers, of their own accord, rose and touched my chest – there, just there where the blood beats – and I was calm.

Oh, but she's here, look. Always was.

THE SECOND DREAM

For the wind passeth over it, and it is gone; and the place thereof shall know it no more. Psalm 103, 16.

I was walking along a lane that seemed to be the old back entry, although there were no walls, and there was muddy ground beneath my feet, rutted as if wheels had passed through it. To the right, where I should have seen the house, there was only long grass and in the grass lay, in their geometric layout, the stone foundations of some long-gone building, the grass growing over them. I stood there and looked down and there was no sound but the repeating sigh of the wind through the grass, over the stone. I said to myself, with a feeling of amazement and the beginning of something like joy:

'Why, look - it's all ancient archaeology now!'